New Headway

Intermediate Teacher's Resource Book

Amanda Maris
Caroline Krantz
Liz and John Soars

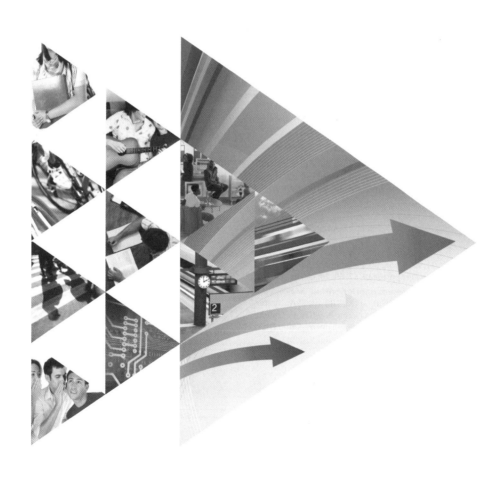

OXFORD
UNIVERSITY PRESS

OXFORD

UNIVERSITY PRESS

Great Clarendon Street, Oxford OX2 6DP

Oxford University Press is a department of the University of Oxford.
It furthers the University's objective of excellence in research, scholarship,
and education by publishing worldwide in

Oxford New York

Auckland Cape Town Dar es Salaam Hong Kong Karachi
Kuala Lumpur Madrid Melbourne Mexico City Nairobi
New Delhi Shanghai Taipei Toronto

With offices in

Argentina Austria Brazil Chile Czech Republic France Greece
Guatemala Hungary Italy Japan Poland Portugal Singapore
South Korea Switzerland Thailand Turkey Ukraine Vietnam

OXFORD and OXFORD ENGLISH are registered trade marks of
Oxford University Press in the UK and in certain other countries

ISBN: 978 0 19 476874 0

Printed in China

ACKNOWLEDGEMENTS

Illustrations by: Gill Button pp.21, 23, 41, 55, 65; Peter Ellis/Meiklejohn
Illustration pp.11, 59, 60; Joanna Kerr pp.15, 49, 67, 69, 70; Gavin Reece p.37

*We would also like to thank the following for permission to reproduce the following
photographs*: Corbis pp.29 (Caterina Bernardi), 71 (Paul Burns); Royalty-free
pp.7 (Ingram), 35 (young woman/Valueline), 35 (young boy/Gareth Boden), 35
(young man with glasses/Photodisc), 35 (older woman/Lifesize/Kathy Quirk-
Syvertsen), 35 (young black man/Blend Images), 51 (Digital Vision)

Introduction

This Teacher's Resource Book contains twenty-nine photocopiable activities and further ideas for you to use with *New Headway Intermediate – Fourth Edition*. It is a new component for the *Headway* series and has been written with two aims in mind:

- to give teachers additional material that revises and extends the work in the Student's Book

- to give students lots of extra speaking practice!

Students at intermediate level need lots of vocabulary and grammar input. Controlled skills work is also important to develop their reading, writing, listening, and speaking. But at the same time, it is also essential that they are given opportunities to 'get active' and actually use their English in meaningful and relevant contexts.

The activities in this book are designed to help your students do this. They encourage students to talk about themselves, compare opinions and views about the world, and practise the kind of situations they are likely to encounter in real life.

In addition, every activity involves an element of team work. Students work together to share or check information, and agree outcomes or solutions. In other words, every activity encourages purposeful interaction where students need to speaak and listen to each other.

Through role plays, language games, questionnaires, and information-gap activities, students are also given the chance to build their confidence and introduce a more personal dimension to their learning.

How to use the photocopiable activities

Each activity starts with the following information:

Lesson link	Suggestion for when to use the worksheet
Aim	The main focus of the activity
Language	The grammar/function exploited
Skills	Speaking, Reading, Writing, and/or Listening
Materials	Notes for preparation of worksheet

Pre-activity

These activities act as a warm-up before students carry out the main activity. They act to remind students of the necessary language needed and to set the context. They are optional, particularly if following straight on from the lesson in the Student's Book.

Procedure

This section has step-by-step instructions for carrying out the main activity. Each main activity takes between fifteen and thirty minutes and is suitable for most class sizes. (There are additional notes for larger classes.) For each activity there is a photocopiable worksheet. Some of the worksheets need to be cut up before handing out to students.

Extension

After each main activity, there is a suggestion for an extension activity. These are generally writing activities which build on the language or topics covered in the main activity. Where this is the case, they can be assigned for homework.

Contents

1.1

How well do you know me?

LESSON LINK Unit 1, SB p9

Aim

To exchange information by playing a board game and talking about your partner

Language

Tenses

Fluency practice

Skills

Speaking and Listening

Materials

One copy of the board game per group of four students. Each group will need a coin and each student will need a counter

Pre-activity (5 minutes)

- Ask students to think of one thing about themselves that other people might find surprising, e.g. *I've eaten snake./I'm going to Australia next month./I have a black belt in karate.*
- Students share the information with the rest of the class. Encourage students to ask follow-up questions.

Procedure (30 minutes)

- Explain that students are going to play a board game in pairs to see how much they can find out about their partner.
- Give each pair of students a copy of the board game, a coin and a counter each. Give them time to read it through and deal with any vocabulary queries.
- Explain that it is not a competitive game but an opportunity to learn as much as you can about your partner.
- Each student begins on a different START spot on the board. Students take it in turns to toss a coin to move round the board (heads = move 1 square, tails = move 2 squares). When they land on a square, they answer the question, giving as much information as they can. If a student lands on a square with a question they have already answered, they move forward to the next square.
- Put students into small groups for a feedback session. Tell them to talk about their partner

Extension (10 minutes)

- Students write down everything that they can remember about a person in the group that they didn't interview. They then pass their paper to that person to check the details are correct.
- If you have time, take in the pieces of paper, read them out aloud, and ask the rest of the class to guess who is being written about.

 START	Where were your parents born?	Why were you given your first name(s)?	START
Have you ever travelled abroad by yourself? Why/Why not?			What interesting things are happening in your life right now?
Where did you go for your last holiday?			Are you a morning person or a night person?
When you were growing up, what was your main ambition?			Did you enjoy being at your first school? Why/Why not?
What's the bravest thing you've ever done?			What's your earliest memory?
Are you an indoor person or an outdoor person?			Do you think life in general is getting easier? Why/Why not?
What's the best piece of advice you've been given by your family?			Where in the world would you most like to visit? Why?
 START	What do you do to relax?	How long have you known your best friend?	START

How well do you know me?

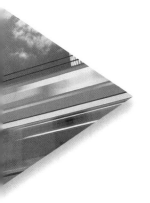

1.2

Aim

To be the first to match words with their descriptions by 'decoding' words in phonetic script

Language

Phonetic script

Pronunciation

Skills

Speaking

Materials

One copy of the worksheet per pair of students

Dictionaries

Answers

1 chat	9 bear
2 April	10 sugar
3 thirty-three	11 shampoo
4 towel	12 sunglasses
5 chemistry	13 boring
6 Japan	14 text message
7 dictionary	15 queen
8 fridge	

HANGMAN

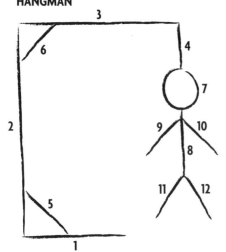

Pre-activity (5 minutes)

- Write the following words on the board and ask students for the pronunciation:
  surfboard / blackboard / message board / cupboard.
- Write the phonetic script of the first three words on the board:
  /ˈsɜːfbɔːd/ /ˈblækbɔːd/ /ˈmesɪdʒbɔːd/
  Underline the sound /ɔː/ in each word and give the pronunciation – point out that it is like the word *or*.
- Ask students to find the correct pronunciation of *cupboard* /ˈkʌbəd/ in a dictionary and highlight the different pronunciation of *board*.
- Give further transcriptions of words with 'difficult' pronunciation and get students to work them out, e.g. *recipe* /ˈresɪpɪ/, *receipt* /reˈsiːt/, *laugh* /lɑːf/, *enough* /ɪˈnʌf/.

Procedure (15 minutes)

- Explain that students are going to have a race to match words in phonetic scripts with their descriptions.
- Put students into pairs and give each pair a worksheet.
- Explain that they have to find a word in phonetics which matches the description and then write the word with its correct spelling. If they get stuck, they should move on quickly to the next question. They have five minutes to complete the task.
- Check the answers when the time limit is up, or when the first pair have finished. Insist on correct pronunciation, encouraging students to self-correct, or get the rest of the class to help them.

Extension (15 minutes)

- Play *Hangman* using phonetic symbols instead of letters. Think of a word, e.g. *computer* /kəmˈpjuːtə/ and write a dash on the board for each of the eight symbols. Students try to guess the word by calling out sounds at random. Write in any correct sounds. Each wrong sound called out makes up one line of the hangman picture. Look at the picture. There are twelve lines in total. The class wins the game if they guess the word before you have finished the picture.

WORDS IN PHONETIC SCRIPT

'taʊəl	beə	kwɪːn
'eɪprəl	ʃæm'puː	t͡ʃæt
θɜːti'θrɪː	'sʌnglɑːsɪz	'kemɪstri
dʒə'pæn	'bɔːrɪŋ	'dɪkʃənri
frɪdʒ	'tekstmesɪdʒ	'ʃʊgə

DESCRIPTIONS

1 talk to your friends   *chat*

2 a month of the year

3 a number

4 something you take to the gym

5 a school subject

6 a country

7 something that can help you learn English

8 something you find in the kitchen

9 an animal that lives in a forest

10 something you can put in tea

11 something you use to wash your hair

12 something you wear

13 an adjective

14 something you can send

15 a member of a royal family

PHONETIC SYMBOLS

vowels	iː	ɪ	ʊ	uː	e	ə	ɜː	ɔː	æ	ʌ	ɑː	ɒ
diphthongs	ɪə	ʊə	eə	eɪ	ɔɪ	aɪ	əʊ	aʊ				
consonants	p	b	t	d	t͡ʃ	dʒ	k	g	f	v	θ	ð
	s	z	ʃ	ʒ	m	n	ŋ	h	l	r	j	w

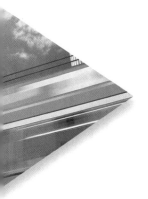

2.1

Aim
To discuss questions related to jobs

Language
Jobs vocabulary

Expressing opinions

Skills
Speaking

Materials
One copy of the worksheet per student

Job vocabulary
firefighter	dentist
referee	vet
surgeon	architect
pop musician	IT engineer
beauty therapist	chef
traffic warden	police officer
actor	soldier
midwife	paramedic

Pre-activity (5 minutes)
- Ask students in small groups to discuss these questions about their own jobs, or the jobs of people they know: *What's your job? Where do you work? When do you start and finish? What do you have to do? Do you enjoy it? Why? Why not?*
- Have a brief class feedback session.

Procedure (20 minutes)
- Give each student a worksheet. Check students know the names of the jobs.
- In their pairs, students discuss the questions. Encourage them to use the language of opinions:

  Expressing opinion: *I reckon … I'd say … I suppose …*

  Agreeing: *I think so too.   Definitely.   Absolutely.*

  Disagreeing: *I'm not so sure.   Actually…*

  Not sure: *Could be.   Maybe, maybe not.   Possibly.*
- When students have finished, ask them to compare their answers with another pair.
- Have a class feedback session. Ask students to think of other jobs which are particularly stressful, well-paid, satisfying, etc.

Extension (15 minutes)
- Write on the board or dictate the following aspects of a job:

  good salary, manageable stress levels, usefulness to society, holidays, opportunities to travel, closeness to home, nice colleagues.

  Ask students individually to rank them in terms of which aspect is most important to them in a job. Then in groups of four, ask them to come up with a group ranking. Have a class feedback session to find the aspects considered most/least important overall.

Background information

Stress: A recent survey suggests that being a firefighter is more stressful than being a sports professional.

The average salary of a surgeon in the UK is £150,000. The average salary of a pop musician is £30,000. In 2009 the highest earning pop artists include U2 (£35 million) and Madonna (£35 million). [www.mirror.co.uk 20.04.09]

Satisfaction: In terms of job satisfaction, art professionals rank 10th out of 60, whilst health professionals rank 13th.

What do you reckon?

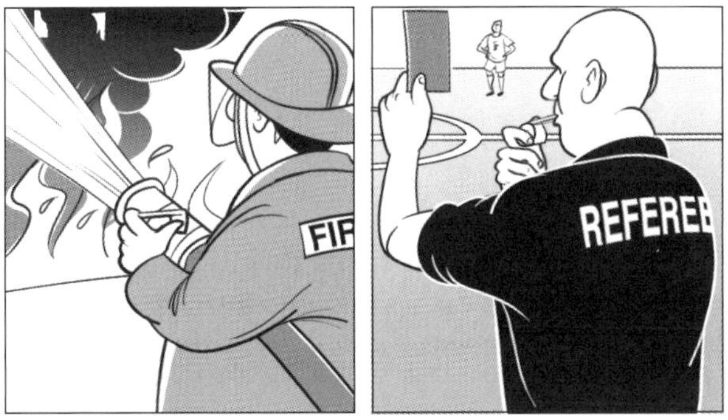

1 Which is more stressful? In what ways?

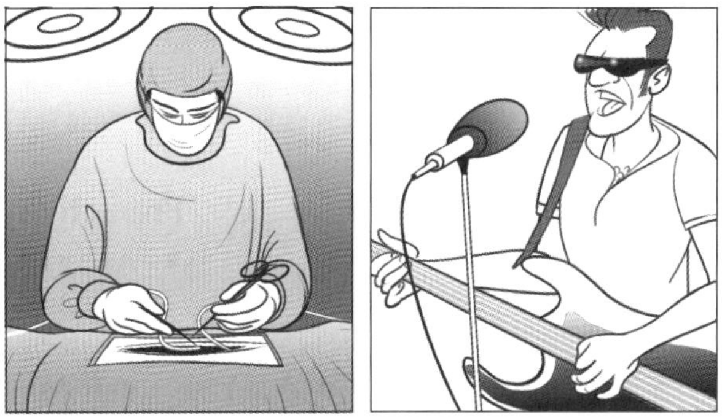

2 Which should be better paid? Give reasons.

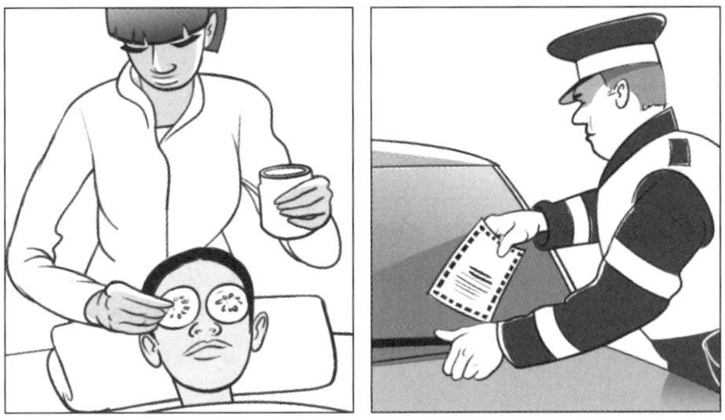

3 Who works harder? Give reasons.

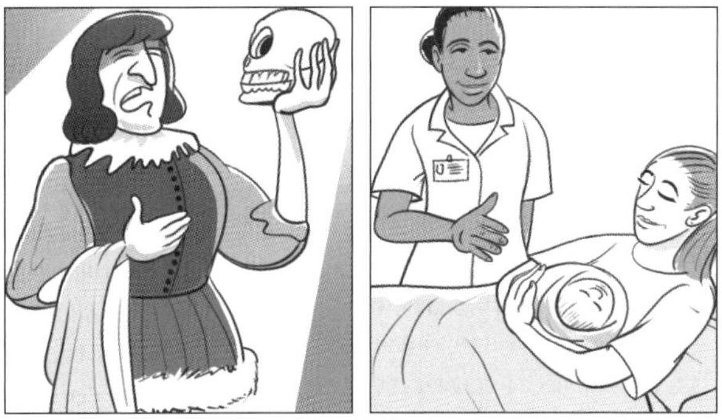

4 Which is more satisfying? In what ways?

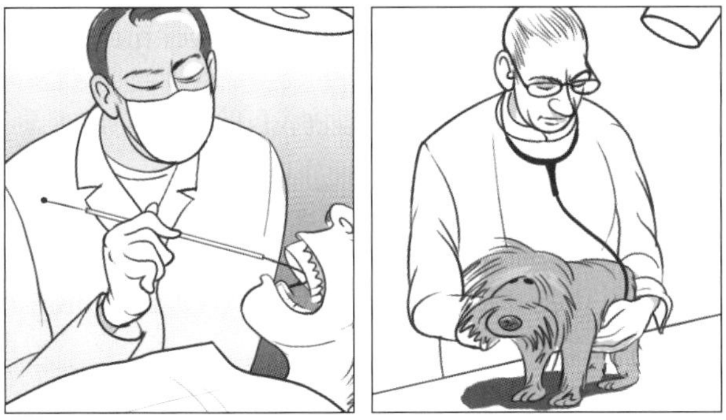

5 Which is more interesting? Give reasons.

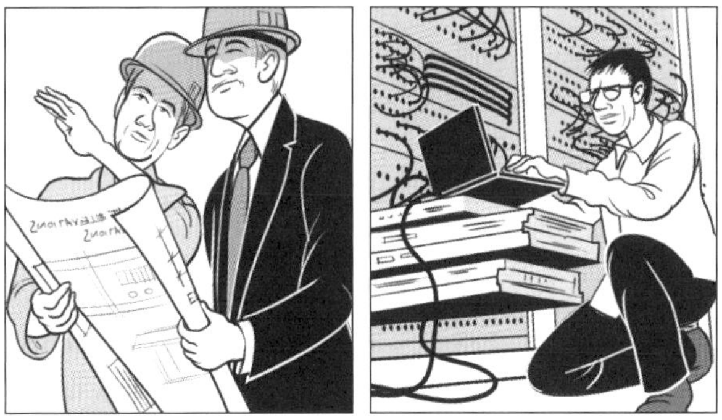

6 Are these done better by a man, a woman, or either? Give reasons.

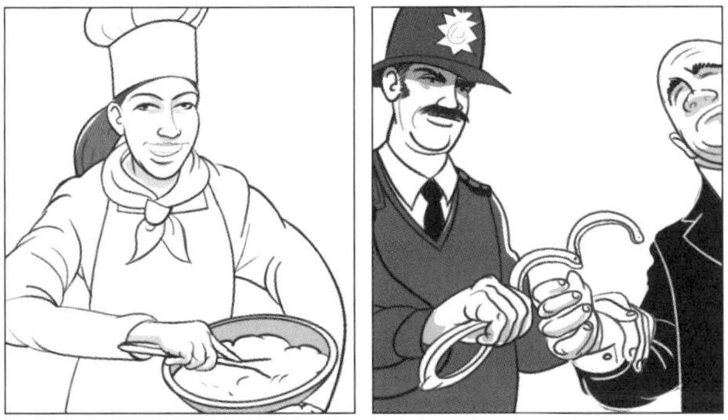

7 Are these done better by an older person, a younger person, or either? Give reasons.

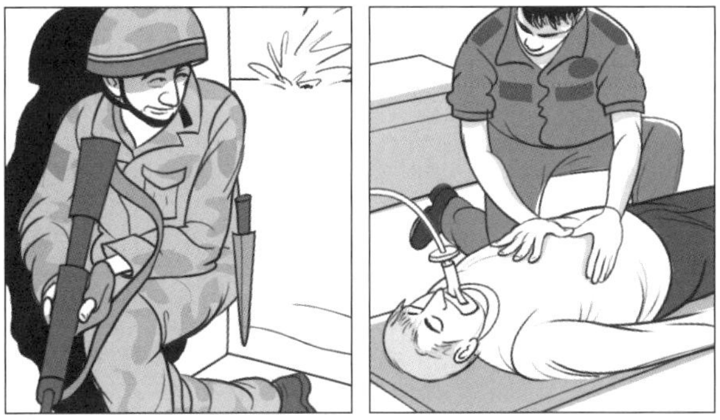

8 Which is more useful to society? In what ways?

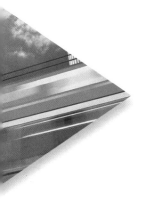

2.2

Aim

To play a board game to talk about work/ studies and free time activities

Language

Present tenses

Free time activities

Fluency practice

Skills

Speaking and Listening

Materials

One copy of the board game and one set of the cards cut up per group of four students. Each group will need a dice and each student will need a counter

Pre-activity (5 minutes)

- Ask students to think about how they spend their time in an average week. Give an example, e.g. *I work just mornings, from about eight till one. In the afternoons, I spend time painting, walking in the hills, and seeing friends.*
- Divide students into pairs to compare their ideas.
- Have a brief feedback session. Establish who would choose a similar timetable.

Procedure (30 minutes)

- Explain that students are going to play a board game about work/ studies and free time activities.
- Divide students into groups of four, two teams of two students. Give each group a copy of the board game, a set of *Quiz* cards, *60 seconds* cards, and *Which activity?* cards placed face down on the table in three piles. Each group will also need a dice and a set of counters.
- Students take it in turns to throw the dice and move round the board. Students take a relevant card and land on one of four possible types of square:

  Quiz: a student from the opposing team asks the player the question on the card

  60 seconds: the player talks about the subject on the card for 60 seconds

  Which activity?: the player describes the activity shown in the photo (without saying the name) for his/her partner to guess

  Bonus/penalty squares: the player moves back/forward according to the instructions

  If a team successfully completes a task, they can stay on their square. If the task is not completed, the team go back one square, but play moves to the other team.

Extension (10 minutes)

- Ask students to make notes about their ideal week. How would they divide their time? Tell students to work in small groups. They should give reasons for their choices.

START ▶

② 60 seconds

③ You work with a colleague/ classmate to get things done. Go forward two spaces.

④ Which activity?

⑧ QUIZ

⑦ You have to work/study all weekend. Go back two spaces.

⑥ QUIZ

⑤ You have so much work that you miss a family party. Go back two spaces.

⑨ 60 seconds

⑩ QUIZ

⑪ Which activity?

⑫ You have the 'Monday morning blues'. Go back two spaces.

⑯ QUIZ

⑮ Which activity?

⑭ You finish all your work early. Go forward two spaces.

⑬ 60 seconds

⑰ Which activity?

⑱ 60 seconds

⑲ QUIZ

⑳ You have a week off with no work to do. Go forward two spaces.

FINISH

㉓ You have to stay late at work/ school. Go back two spaces.

㉒ Which activity?

㉑ 60 seconds

? QUIZ ?

Q In which sport do you serve an ace?

A Tennis.

? QUIZ ?

Q What does DIY stand for?

A Do-it-yourself.

 60 seconds

What are you doing at work/school/university at the moment?

? QUIZ ?

Q What do you use to give you light when you're camping?

A A torch.

? QUIZ ?

Q What do you use to make a hole in a wall?

A A drill.

 60 seconds

An average day at work/school/university

? QUIZ ?

Q Who uses a zoom?

A A photographer?

? QUIZ ?

Q How do you cook a cake: roast it or bake it?

A Bake it.

 60 seconds

How many hours do people work/study in your country?

? QUIZ ?

Q What does an artist do with a pencil?

A Sketch.

? QUIZ ?

Q What do cyclists wear to protect their head?

A A helmet.

 60 seconds

The best thing about your work/studies

? QUIZ ?

Q What do people do when they do yoga?

A Meditate.

? QUIZ ?

Q What do you usually do first with vegetables, peel or chop them?

A Peel them.

 60 seconds

The worst thing about your work/studies

? QUIZ ?

Q What do you use in tennis: a bat or a racket?

A A racket.

? QUIZ ?

Q Where do people go to get a bargain?

A The sales.

 60 seconds

Your ideal job

60 seconds

Your favourite day of the week

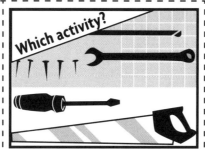 Which activity?

 Which activity?

 60 seconds

How you spend your weekends?

 Which activity?

 Which activity?

 60 seconds

What do you like about your favourite hobby?

 Which activity?

 Which activity?

 60 seconds

A free time activity that you do regularly

 Which activity?

 Which activity?

 60 seconds

A hobby popular with young people in your country at the moment

 Which activity?

 Which activity?

 60 seconds

Your favourite recipe

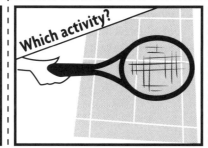 Which activity?

 Which activity?

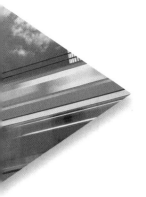

3.1

Life's highs and lows

LESSON LINK Unit 3, SB p23

Aim
To create an imaginary life using prompts

Language
Past tenses

Time expressions

Skills
Speaking and Listening

Materials
One copy of the worksheet cut up into cards per pair of students

Pre-activity (10 minutes)

- Brainstorm life events with the class and write them on the board, e.g. *pass exams, leave school, get a job, get married, buy a house/ flat, retire,* etc.
- Divide students into small groups. Ask them to put the life events on the board in a logical order.
- Have a brief feedback session.

Procedure (30 minutes)

- Explain that students are going to create the life story of a man called Dan Marshall starting from the day he left school.
- Put students into pairs and give each pair a set of cards. Students spread out the cards face down.
- Each pair chooses 10 cards from the set.
- Students turn the cards over. Explain that they describe 10 events in Dan Marshall's life. Ask students to read the cards and check any new vocabulary. You may need to pre-teach/check the following: *voluntary work, to fall out with someone, identity theft, to be an extra in a film, to inherit money.*
  Students work in their pairs to order the life events in a logical way and number the cards 1–10.
- In their pairs, students create Dan's life story using the events in the order they have numbered them. Encourage students to add more details for each event and to use time expressions and linkers e.g. *Unfortunately… While…, Before he had…* etc. to make the story flow more logically. They should take notes to help them remember the key points, but should not write the story in full.
- Put the students into new pairs and ask them to take turns to tell Dan's life story to their new partner. They should compare their stories.
- Have a class feedback session. Ask individual students to tell you their partner's account of Dan's life. Establish who created the most interesting life story.

Extension (10 minutes)

- Tell students they are going to invent a character (name, age, gender) and tell his/her life around the class. Each student thinks of a life event and writes it down without showing anyone. Students take it in turns to include their event in telling the character's life story.

He got a job in Information Technology.	He set up his own business on the Internet.
He bought a six-bedroomed house.	He took up painting and sketching.
He did a year's voluntary work.	He went to university.
He was a victim of identity theft.	He lost a lot of money.
He was involved in a skiing accident.	He was an extra in a film.
He fell in love.	He fell out with his family.
He went to live in South America.	He inherited some money from his grandparents.
He got married.	He retired.
He travelled round Europe for six months.	He was arrested.

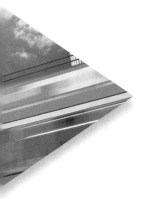

3.2

Aim

To play a board game to revise the form and uses of the verbs in Unit 3

Language

Past Simple, Past Continuous, Past Perfect, and *used to*

Skills

Speaking

Materials

One copy of the snakes and ladders board per group and one copy of the Answers for each referee

Each group of students will need a dice and counters

Pre-activity (5 minutes)

- Briefly review the past forms of the Past Simple, Past Continuous, Past Perfect Simple and Continuous, and *used to* by putting these prompts on the board and asking students to complete them.
  By the time I left school, I'd been –ing …
  I used to …
  Yesterday when I woke up, the sun was …ing …

Procedure (20 minutes)

- Explain that students are going to play a game of snakes and ladders to practise the Past Simple, Past Continuous, Past Perfect and *used to*.
- Put students into groups of three or more and give each group a copy of the worksheet, a dice, and counters. Point out that on the board there are prompts and snakes and ladders. Make one student the referee, and give them a copy of the answers. The referee does not let the other students see the answers.
- When a student lands on a square they should make a full sentence from the prompts with the correct past forms of the verbs. The referee uses the Answer sheet to decide if the answer is correct. If the answer is correct, they can throw the dice again. If the answer is not correct, the player's turn ends. (The referee should not say the correct answer in case another player lands on the square.)
- If a player lands on a square with a ladder, they move to the top of the ladder, but only if they have answered the question at the bottom correctly. If the player lands on a snake's head, they move to the bottom of the snake and wait until their next turn before throwing again.

Extension (15 minutes)

- Ask students to work in pairs and choose one of the sentences in the task as the start to a short story/anecdote. Students write notes for the key events in the story
- Students work with a new partner and tell each other their story/anecdote.

SNAKES AND LADDERS

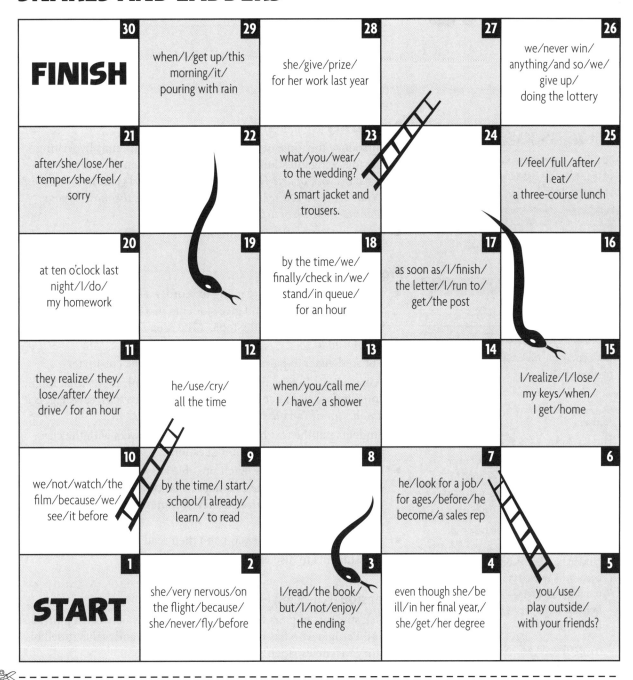

Answers

2 She was very nervous on the flight because she'd never flown before.
3 I read the book but I didn't enjoy the ending.
4 Even though she'd been ill in her final year, she got her degree.
5 Did you use to play outside with your friends?
7 He'd been looking for a job for ages before he became a sales rep.
9 By the time I'd started school, I'd already learnt to read.
10 We didn't watch the film because we'd seen it before.
11 They realized they were lost after they'd been driving/ they'd driven for an hour.
12 He used to cry all the time.
13 When you called me, I was having a shower.
15 I realized I'd lost my keys when I got home.

17 As soon as I'd finished the letter, I ran to get the last post.
18 By the time we finally checked in, we'd been standing in a queue for an hour.
20 At ten o'clock last night I was doing my homework.
21 After she lost her temper, she felt sorry.
23 What did you wear to the wedding?
   A smart jacket and trousers.
25 I felt really full after I'd eaten a three-course lunch.
26 We'd never won anything and so we gave up doing the lottery.
28 She was given a prize for her work last year.
29 When I got up this morning, it was pouring with rain.

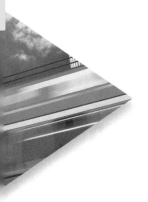

3.3

The theft of the *Mona Lisa*

LESSON LINK Unit 3, SB p24

Answers

1 j 2 f 3 a 4 g 5 c 6 e 7 b 8 i 9 h 10 d

1 Perugia said he stole the work out of patriotism. He thought a painting by an Italian painter belonged in an Italian gallery.

2 He had spent Sunday night hiding in a small, dark room in the museum. Early on Monday morning, before the museum opened, he entered the room where the painting was hanging and took it down from the wall. Then he cut the painting from its frame.

3 As the museum was still locked, he unscrewed the door handle and escaped. He'd kept the painting for more than two years before he took it to the Uffizi Gallery in Florence.

4 Perugia was a national hero. He was sent to prison, but people sent letters and bottles of wine to his cell, and women baked cakes for him. He was given a reduced sentence of seven months. By that time, he'd already been in jail for nearly eight months and so he was released.

Pre-activity (5 minutes)

● Introduce the topic of art and art galleries/museums by writing the following questions on the board: *Have you got a favourite artist or work of art? How often do you visit art galleries/museums? What art have you seen? What do you think is the most famous painting or work of art in the world?*

● Students discuss the questions in pairs or small groups.

Procedure (30 minutes)

● Explain that students are going to reorder a text. Write the title of the text on the board and give students two minutes to brainstorm what they know about the topic. (The *Mona Lisa* is also known as *La Giaconda*.)

● Put students into pairs and give each group the cut-up text.

● Ask students to look at the sentences and think about what might come before and after the parts of the sentence they have, e.g. *Is it a noun/a verb/an auxiliary? Is it active/passive?*

● Students put the text in order. Check the answers with the class and ask a few comprehension questions.

● Hand out the questions. Elicit possible answers to the first one. Encourage students to use *Perhaps …, Maybe …, It's possible that …* in their answers. Give groups a few minutes to discuss questions 2–4.

● Have a class feedback session and then read out the answers.

● Ask students to discuss question 5.

Extension (15 minutes)

● Ask students in pairs to role play an interview between a journalist and Perugia who has just come out of prison and wants to sell his story to a newspaper.

j On Monday, August 21, 1911, the world's most famous work of art, Leonardo da Vinci's *Mona Lisa*, was

e gone! The police were contacted immediately and the museum was closed for a week while the theft was thoroughly

f stolen from the Louvre museum in Paris. The next day a man called Louis Béroud went to the museum. He was a painter and at that time he was

b investigated. When the news was made public, it became an international sensation. Many people who worked at or near the museum, were questioned

a painting a picture of the gallery. He noticed that the painting wasn't hanging in its usual place. He immediately contacted

i by the police, including Pablo Picasso because he had bought two sculptures from a friend who had actually

g the security guard but the guard thought that the museum's official photographer had

h stolen them from the Louvre a few months before. After an interrogation, the police decided that Picasso knew nothing about the theft of the *Mona Lisa*. Luckily, the painting was

c taken it off the wall to take pictures of it in his studio. The guard went to the studio to check but found that it wasn't there either – the painting had

d found 27 months later. An Italian man, Vincenzo Perugia, was arrested as he tried to sell it to the Uffizi Gallery in Florence, Italy.

What do you think?

1 Why do you think Perugia stole the paintings?
2 How do you think he got into the museum?
3 How do you think he got out of the museum?
4 What do you think the punishment for his crime was?
5 What do you think about Perugia, his crime, and the punishment?

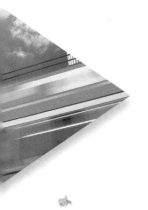

4.1

Aim

To discuss personal experiences and opinions

Language

Phrasal verbs

Questions forms

Fluency practice

Skills

Speaking

Materials

One copy of the worksheet per pair of students

Answers

1 h		6 d	
2 e		7 b	
3 j		8 f	
4 a		9 i	
5 c		10 g	

Pre-activity (5 minutes)

- Review the phrasal verbs from Unit 4 by calling out a phrasal verb with the wrong preposition and getting students to correct it, e.g. *give off (up) chocolate for a month*
- Elicit a few personal examples from the class with the verbs in context, e.g. *I should give up smoking. The person I take after is my grandfather.*

Procedure (20 minutes)

- Explain that students are going to interview each other about personal experiences and people they know.
- Put the students into pairs. Give each pair a copy of the worksheet.
- Ask students, in their pairs, to match the cartoons with the topics.
- Explain that students are now going to interview each other about five of the topics in the list. Students choose five different topics each.
- Tell students they are going to interview each other. Encourage them to continue the conversation each time e.g.

  A *Have you given up a bad habit recently?*

  B *Yes, I've given up taking sugar in my coffee. What about you?*

  A *I haven't given up anything. I don't have any bad habits!*
- Have a class feedback session. Invite students to tell the class anything interesting they found about their partner.

Extension (20 minutes)

- Ask students to write a short story using as many of the phrasal verbs in the worksheet as possible. Give them the opening sentence: *The Browns moved to Texas and brought up their children on a cattle ranch.*
- Display all the stories on the classroom wall. Give students time to read each other's work. If appropriate, students can vote for the one they like best.

What about you?

1 Match the conversation topics (1–10) with the cartoons (a–j).

1		a bad habit that you have given up recently
2		a child who has been well brought up
3		a hobby you would like to take up
4		a person you take after
5		a difficult thing you have to get through
6		the last time somebody looked after you
7		a person you don't get on with very well
8		something you are really looking forward to
9		the best way to pick up a foreign language
10		something bad you have to put up with

2 Choose five topics and discuss them with a partner.

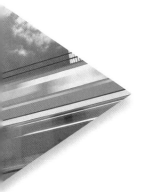

4.2

Aim

To play a quiz game about customs in different cultures

Language

Modal verbs of obligation

Skills

Reading, Writing, Speaking, and Listening

Materials

One copy of the worksheet cut into cards per group of four students

Pre-activity (5 minutes)

- Introduce the topic of customs and traditions by asking the students what they do on the following days: *their birthday, a national holiday, New Year's Day*, etc. Do they have any customs which are special to their country or region?

Procedure (30 minutes)

- Explain that students are going to play a quiz game where they guess the customs of different countries around the world.

  Show students how the game works by writing an example on the board: *In Japan you should greet someone (a) by shaking hands (b) with a nod and a bow (c) with a kiss on the cheek.* Elicit the answer (b).

- Put students into four teams. Give Team A worksheet A, Team B worksheet B and so on. (If you have a large class, divide students into eight teams.)

- Students work in their teams and brainstorm two possible but incorrect options for each question of their worksheet.

- Pair two teams with different worksheets together to play the game. Sitting opposite each other, teams take it in turns to read out the customs and the three possible answers. The students in the other team discuss the options and choose the answer they think is correct. The team who is guessing bets 1, 2, or 3 points on their chosen answer depending on how confident they are that it is correct. If they guess correctly, they keep the points; if they guess incorrectly, they lose the points. The team with the most points at the end wins.

- Have a class feedback session to find out which customs students found most interesting/surprising.

Extension (15 minutes)

- Ask students to produce a leaflet for visitors to their country with advice on how to behave. Write the following headings on the board and brainstorm ideas and examples for each category: *greeting people, eating in restaurants, visiting people's homes, shopping, giving gifts, body language and gestures.* Give students time to write their leaflet.

- Display all the leaflets on the classroom walls and give students time to read each other's work.

A Call my cultural bluff

1 In China, you shouldn't leave your chopsticks:

 a standing up in a bowl of rice.

 b _____

 c _____

2 The Spanish have a special way of celebrating New Year. At midnight on New Year's Eve they:

 a _____

 b eat twelve grapes, one for each chime of the clock.

 c _____

3 When you enter someone's home in Finland, you should:

 a take off your shoes.

 b _____

 c _____

4 In Belgium, the number of 'air kisses' people expect when they greet each other is:

 a _____

 b _____

 c three.

B Call my cultural bluff

1 In Italy, you should drink cappuccino coffee:

 a _____

 b _____

 c only at breakfast.

2 If you want to give someone flowers in France, you should:

 a _____

 b give odd numbers but not 13 (this is considered unlucky).

 c _____

3 In Greece, the unluckiest combination of day and date is:

 a Tuesday the 13th.

 b _____

 c _____

4 In Bulgaria, you have to be careful with body language. For example:

 a a nod means 'no' and a shake of the head means 'yes'.

 b _____

 c _____

C Call my cultural bluff

1 If invited to dinner or a social event in Mexico, it's acceptable to:

 a arrive 30 minutes late.

 b _____

 c _____

2 If you are in a public place in Japan, you shouldn't:

 a _____

 b blow your nose.

 c _____

3 In Scotland on the 25th January, people have a Burn's Supper to celebrate their national:

 a _____

 b poet.

 c _____

4 In Turkey, it's considered rude to point to:

 a _____

 b _____

 c the sole of your foot towards another person.

D Call my cultural bluff

1 In a traditional British wedding, the bride carries or wears:

 a something old, something new, something borrowed, and something blue.

 b _____

 c _____

2 In India, the Western gesture of waving to say hello may be interpreted as:

 a _____

 b _____

 c go away.

3 In Thailand, you shouldn't touch anyone, even a child on:

 a _____

 b the head (it's considered sacred).

 c _____

4 In restaurants in the USA, you won't be well thought of if you don't:

 a _____

 b _____

 c leave a tip of ten or fifteen per cent.

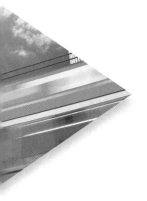

5.1

Building a better future

LESSON LINK   Unit 5, SB p39

Aim

To build words in a personalized pair work activity

Language

Suffixes and prefixes

Skills

Speaking

Materials

One copy of the worksheet per pair of students

Answers

Pre-activity

behave – behaviour, misbehave, well-behaved, badly-behaved

imagine – imagination, imaginary, imaginative, imaginatively

responsible – responsibility, responsibly, irresponsible, irresponsibility, irresponsibly

Main activity

A	B
1 employers	1 arrangements
2 suitable	2 creative
3 disappear	3 extra-terrestrial
4 automatically	4 happiness
5 useful	5 agreement
6 regularly	6 reaction
7 predictions	7 actively
8 successful	8 expensive

Pre-activity (10 minutes)

- Write the word *excite* on the board. Elicit prefixes and suffixes that can be used to build more words:
  excitement / *exciting* / *excited* / *excitedly* / *unexciting*
- Write the following words on the board:
  behave   imagine   responsible
- Students work in groups of three and build as many words as possible from the base, using dictionaries if appropriate.
- Check the answers and decide which group has built the most words.

Procedure (20 minutes)

- Explain that students are going to build words to complete questions about the future and then interview a partner.
- Divide the students into pairs. Give Students A worksheet A and Students B worksheet B. Explain that A and B have different questions and remind students not to show each other their worksheets.
- Students work individually to build the words and complete the questions. Remind them that they need to add a suffix/prefix to all the words in brackets. Allow students to use dictionaries if appropriate. (You could get students to work in A/A and B/B pairs during this stage.)
- Explain that students are now going to interview each other using the questions on their worksheet
- Students interview each other. Encourage them to ask as many follow-up questions as possible and to give reasons for their answers.
- Have a class feedback session. Invite students to tell the class anything interesting they discussed with their partner.

Extension (15 minutes)

- Ask students to take five words each from the vocabulary section on p39 of the Student's Book.
- Students work in pairs and ask their partner their questions.

Building a better future

Complete the questions with the correct form of the word in brackets.

1 What skills do you think _____ will be looking for in the future? **EMPLOY**

2 How do you think cities will change to make them _____ for the challenges of the future? **SUIT**

3 Which species of animal do you think might _____ in the next fifty years? **APPEAR**

4 Do you think housework will be done _____ by robots in houses of the future? **AUTOMATIC**

5 What gadgets do you think will be invented in the future? How will they be _____ ? **USE**

6 What small things do you do _____ to help the environment? **REGULAR**

7 Do you believe scientists' _____ about global warming? Why/Why not? **PREDICT**

8 In what ways would you like to be _____ in the future? **SUCCESS**

Ask and answer the questions with a partner.

- -

Building a better future

Complete the questions with the correct form of the word in brackets.

1 What _____ should people make for a happy retirement? **ARRANGE**

2 What do think will be more important in the future, practical skills or a _____ mind? **CREATE**

3 Do you think humans will make contact with _____ beings in the future? **TERRESTRIAL**

4 What's your idea of perfect _____ for the future? **HAPPY**

5 How can we encourage _____ between different countries about the future of the Earth? **AGREE**

6 What's your _____ when people say we should ban air travel? **REACT**

7 Would you _____ take part in an environmental campaign in your town/city? Why/Why not? **ACTIVE**

8 What everyday things do you think will become more _____ in the future? **EXPENSE**

Ask and answer the questions with a partner.

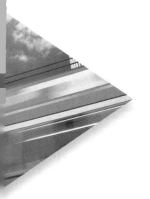

5.2

Aim

To discuss making everyday changes to improve your life and to make an action plan

Language

Future forms and *might*

Fluency

Skills

Speaking

Materials

One copy of the worksheet per student

Pre-activity (5 minutes)

- Write the following question on the board: *Are you a creature of habit or do you enjoy making changes?* Answer the question yourself, giving examples from your own experience.
- Elicit students' answers in a brief class discussion.

Procedure (30 minutes)

- Explain that students are going to look at a list of simple ways of making changes and improving everyday life/protecting the planet.
- Give each student a copy of the worksheet.
- Students choose five of the changes that they would like to make in their own life and think about the reasons for their choices.
- Put students into groups of four. Students take it in turns to present their choice to the rest of the group, giving reasons to justify their selection.
- Students then work together in their groups to select the most important four changes they would like to include in an action plan. Point out that all four students must agree on the final selection.
- Put students into new groups of four to present their action plan to some of the other students.
- Have a class feedback session to find out what the most popular changes are and compile an action plan of five changes for the whole class.

Extension (10 minutes)

- Ask students to work in pairs or small groups and to think of three more changes they can make to break the routine or improve their world. Ask them to prepare an action plan with ideas on how to get others to agree to their suggestions and present it to the rest of the class.

Easy ways to the feel-good factor

In today's 24/7 society it's easy to get stuck in a routine and do the same things week in, week out. We all have a few bad habits, but you don't need to turn your world upside down to make changes. Here are fourteen easy ways to get the feel-good factor – for you, your town, and for the planet.

1 I think I'll try to catch up with a friend I haven't seen for ages.

2 I'm going to always put my chewing gum in the bin.

3 I'm going to turn my central heating thermostat down by 1°.

4 I'm going to fly less often.

5 I might become a blood donor.

6 I'll try to buy food from my local region.

7 I might walk or ride my bike for journeys of 2km or less.

8 I might take up something creative like painting or poetry.

9 I'll try to stop worrying about what I can't change.

10 I think I'll try a 'staycation' this year – a holiday in which you stay at home, relax, and enjoy what your local area has to offer.

11 I'm going to have a tech-free day once a week – no computers, email, iPods, or TV – just real communication.

12 I might join a local volunteer group and improve the look of my town.

13 I'm going to try to spend time with someone much older or younger than me.

14 I'm going to try and get more sleep.

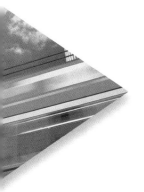

5.3

Aim
To match key words with their stress patterns

Language
Word stress

Skills
Speaking

Materials
One copy of the worksheet per student

Answers

Pre-activity

oOoo laboratory

Ooo confident

ooOo television

oOo excitement

Main task

1 oOoo
impossible / irregular / librarian / advertisement / photographer

2 Ooo
happiness / consciousness / colourful / usefulness / advertise

3 ooOo
disagreement / explanation / inexpensive / operation / unsuccessful

4 oOo
imagine / employer / reaction / unkindness / creative

Pre-activity (5 minutes)

- Write the following words and stress patterns on the board:
  excitement / confident / laboratory / television
     oOoo   Ooo   ooOo   oOo

- Ask a student to come to the board and match them. Allow other students to check/correct the pairings before you confirm the answers.

Procedure (15 minutes)

- Explain that students are going to have a race to practise the word stress patterns on the board.

- Give each student a copy of the worksheet. Explain that they have to match the stress pattern on each rocket to the correct word on the planets. They then have to plot the correct route through the stars for each rocket by choosing the words that have the same stress pattern.

- Put students into pairs to do the race. Set a time limit of five minutes, and tell students to begin. Encourage them to say the words aloud as this will help them. Students write the answers under the rockets.

- The first pair to finish the race with all the correct answers are the winners.

- Check the answers and pronunciation with the class. Drill the pronunciation if students have problems.

Extension (10 minutes)

- Put students into new pairs. Each pair chooses a stress pattern, either from this activity or a new pattern, and finds eight words from Units 1–5 that fit that pattern and four that don't. Students write the words muddled up on a piece of paper and exchange papers with another pair. They then decide which words fit the stress pattern.

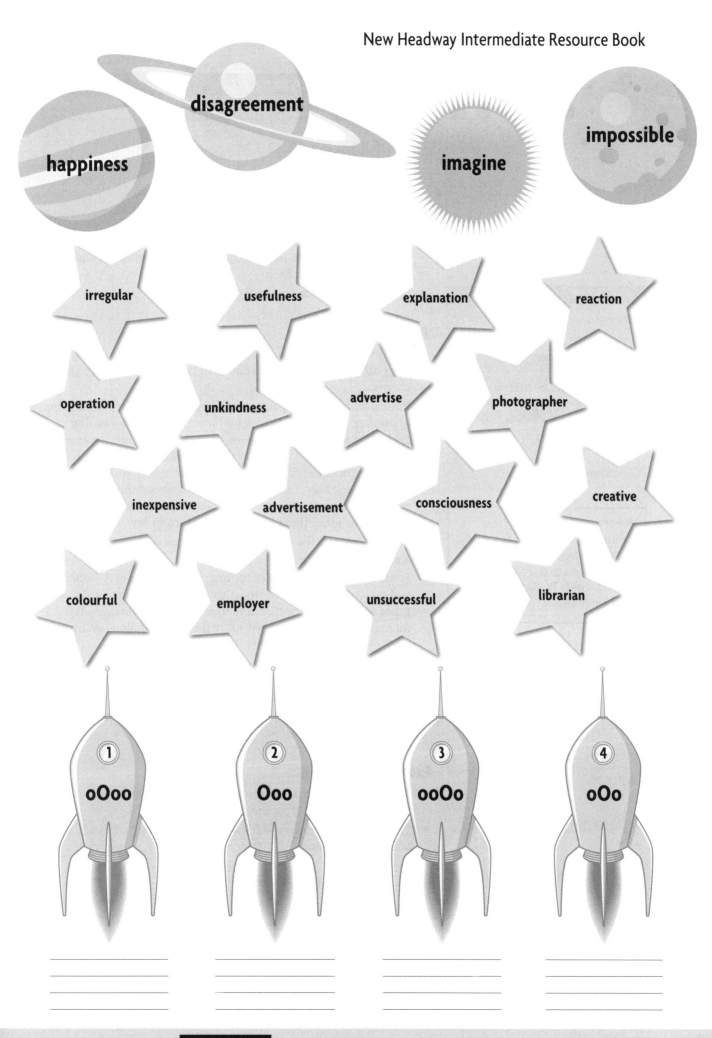

disagreement

happiness

imagine

impossible

irregular

usefulness

explanation

reaction

operation

unkindness

advertise

photographer

inexpensive

advertisement

consciousness

creative

colourful

employer

unsuccessful

librarian

1 oOoo

2 Ooo

3 ooOo

4 oOo

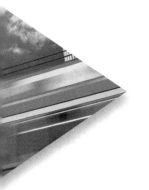

6.1

Aim

To write an advert and roleplay a presentation to a client

Language

Adjectives

Fluency practice

Skills

Speaking, Listening, and Writing

Materials

One copy of worksheets cut up per pair of students

Dictionaries

Mini-project idea

The material in this unit could be used as part of a mini-project on advertising. You could bring in examples of print adverts or show a range of TV adverts before the advert writing stage.

Pre-activity (5 minutes)

- Introduce the topic of advertising by describing an advert (on TV, radio, the Internet, or in print) that you think is effective and one that you think is irritating.
- Students do the same in small groups.

Procedure (40 minutes)

- Explain that students work for an advertising agency called *Flash*. They are going to prepare an advert in pairs and present it to their clients.
- Put students into A/A pairs and B/B pairs. The A/A pairs are going to prepare an advert for a new perfume using the information given, and B/B students are going to prepare an advert for a new brand of trainers. Give the A Students worksheet A and the B Students worksheet B. Allow students time to read through their relevant worksheet. Explain that they have already brainstormed possible names and slogans. They should choose the name and the slogan which they think best fit the product, or invent new ones.
- Students prepare their adverts. Allow the use of dictionaries, if appropriate.
- For the presentation stage of the task, put two pairs of A students and two pairs of B students together to make a group of eight. If possible, arrange the furniture to make the presentation stage more realistic. The A students make their presentations in turn to the B students who are clients. They have only five minutes each time. The clients vote for the advert they like best.
- Students change roles with the B students presenting in turn and the A students playing the clients.
- Students choose the best one or two adverts from the whole class in a brief feedback session.

Extension (15 minutes)

- Students work in two teams, one brainstorming the pros of advertising and the other the cons.
- Students have a debate and try to persuade the opposite team to accept their opinions.

Worksheet A

FLASH

Advert profile

Name: _____

Slogan: _____

Wording for magazine ad: _____

_____

_____

_____

_____

Packaging materials: _____

Colour: _____

What product says about the user: _____

How different from competition: _____

Celebrity endorsement

Name: _____

Reason: _____

Music for campaign: _____

Possible additional products: _____

Possible names
Elegance
Summer
Sunrise
Silk

Possible slogans
- A fresh fragrance, a fresh idea for a new you
- The coolest fragrance you'll ever try
- Be distinctive Be yourself
- Naturally

Worksheet B

FLASH

Advert profile

Name: _____

Slogan: _____

Wording for magazine ad: _____

_____

_____

_____

Packaging materials: _____

Colour: _____

What product says about the user: _____

How different from competition: _____

Celebrity endorsement

Name: _____

Reason: _____

Music for campaign: _____

Possible additional products: _____

Possible names
Street nation
Identity
Kings of cool
No limits

Possible slogans
- The only ID you'll ever need
- State-of-the-art from head to toe
- For life in techno-colour

6.2

What matters most to me

LESSON LINK   Unit 6, SB p49

Pre-activity (5 minutes)

- Write the following ages on the board: 6, 17, 35, 53, and 76. Ask students *What do you think matters most at these different ages?* Elicit a range of answers, *e.g. At six, things like having toys and playing matters a lot. At 76, staying in good health is important.*

Procedure (30 minutes)

- Explain that students are going to discuss what matters most to people by reading a range of responses in a magazine article, completing a diagram with their own priorities, and then comparing with a classmate.
- Give each student a copy of the worksheet and allow a few minutes for them to read the first responses.
- Put students into pairs. Focus on what matters most to Harry (*my children*).
- Students then take it in turns to read out the opinions in the article to each other, and decide what matters most to each person. Check the answers with the class.
- Write a list of the five most important things to you on the board. Explain your choices using some of the language on the worksheet.
- Elicit examples for each of the sentence starters. Encourage students to sound expressive.
- Put students in new pairs to summarize their lists and compare their ideas.
- Ask students to report back on anything interesting they found out about their partner in a brief feedback session.

Extension (15 minutes)

- Ask students to choose one of the people/things that matters to them most and write a diary entry about him/her/it. They can focus on the last time they saw a person, did an activity, or used an object.

1

What matters most to me

Harry	children

They're everything to me. The day they were born completely changed my life. And they're the future, aren't they?

Magda	

I take it everywhere. It contains my whole life and I use it for everything from booking tickets to looking for a new job. And it's light enough to carry anywhere.

Leo	

I don't want to sound selfish or anything, but you can't really live without it. I work very hard and I expect to be rewarded. And I like the finer things in life. What's wrong with that?

Andy	

My Dad and I have never missed a match. There's nothing like standing with the crowd of supporters cheering on the lads.

Sylvie	

I'm a widow and I live alone and so she's company for me. Plus she's good security. Every time the doorbell rings she starts barking very loud.

Mark	

I'll never forget the day we met at primary school. Even though we don't see each other very often, we still get on like a house on fire.

Kelly	

I saw it in the showroom and just had to have it – in bright red of course! The thing I love about it is the speed: nought to sixty in under ten seconds.

Yuko	

I get to travel a lot and meet all sorts of interesting people. It isn't that well paid, but money isn't everything, is it?

Tim	

It's small but really cosy and with a wonderful view of the river. We only moved there a month ago but we've settled in really quickly.

Paula	

I just couldn't live without them. I've got shelves full of them at home and I go to the library every week. I love the way they show you so many different worlds.

2 Write the five things that matter most to you.

1 _____

2 _____

3 _____

4 _____

5 _____

Use the expressions to discuss them with a partner.

I just couldn't live without …

… mean(s) the world to me.

I love the way he/she/they …

… isn't everything, is it?

The thing/What I love about … is …

There's nothing like …

I'll never forget the day …

What I don't understand is why …

I can't get over …

… is everything to me.

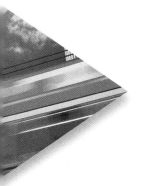

6.3

Aim

To describe pictures and find 12 differences

Language

Department store vocabulary

Describing the details of a scene

Skills

Speaking

Materials

One copy of the worksheet cut in half per pair of students

Answers

In A, toys and babywear, sports, and luggage are on the third floor. In B, they are on the second floor.

In A, there isn't a hairdresser's on the first floor. In B, there is.

In A, linen is in the basement. In B it's on the first floor.

In A, bathroom accessories are in the basement. In B, they're on the ground floor.

In A, the escalator is going down. In B, it's going up.

In A, a woman is picking up a trolley case. In B, a teenage boy is picking up a holdall. (2 differences).

In A, a man is buying a tennis racket. In B, he's buying a pair of trainers.

In A, the man is paying by credit card. In B, he's paying with cash.

In A, the bag says the sale end on 30th June. In B, it says it ends on 31st July.

In A, the offer is golf balls: buy two packs for £20. In B, it's for sport socks: buy 2 pairs, get 1 free.

In A, there's a sign for customer services. In B, there's a sign to the cafeteria.

Pre-activity (10 minutes)

- Review the language of department stores by saying the names of different items on a shopping list and eliciting the correct department. e.g. *a bedside table* (furniture), *a teddy bear* (toys), *towels* (linen), *a frying pan* (kitchenware). You could do this as a competition. Divide students into teams. Write your shopping list on the board or dictate it. The first team to write down all the correct departments is the winner.

Procedure (20 minutes)

- Explain that students are going to work together to find the differences in a pair of similar pictures of a department in a store.
- Put students into pairs. Give Students A worksheet A, and Students B worksheet B, and tell them they must not show each other their picture. Explain that students need to find 12 differences by describing details and asking questions about each picture.
- In pairs, students take it in turns to describe and ask questions about their picture. They should focus on the people/objects and also the signs. When they find a difference, they draw a circle round it.
- The first pair to find all the differences is the winning pair. When everyone has finished, have a class feedback session to go through all the differences.

Extension (10 minutes)

- Students look back at their picture and draw in some extra detail in any of the clear spaces. They can add in people, objects, signs, information about special offers, etc.
- Students work with a new partner and remind them they must not show each other their picture. Students take it in turns to describe what they have added to their picture while their partner draws in the detail.
- When students have finished, they compare their pictures to see how well they have exchanged the information.

Worksheet A

STORE GUIDE

3 Third floor
Toys and
babywear
Sports
Luggage

2 Second floor
Stationery
TV, audio, and
phones
Electrical
appliances

1 First floor
Ladies' fashions
Lingerie
Menswear

G Ground floor
Jewellery
Cosmetics
Toiletries
Leather goods

B Basement
Furniture
China and
glassware
Kitchenware
Bathroom
accessories
Linen

Worksheet B

STORE GUIDE

3 Third floor
Stationery
TV, audio, and
phones
Electrical
appliances

2 Second floor
Toys and
babywear
Sports
Luggage

1 First floor
Hairdresser's
Ladies' fashions
Lingerie
Menswear
Linen

G Ground floor
Jewellery
Cosmetics
Toiletries
Bathroom
accessories
Leather goods

B Basement
Furniture
China and
glassware
Kitchenware

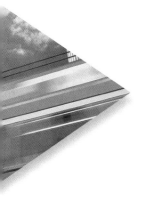

7.1

It's a matter of opinion
LESSON LINK   Unit 7, SB p57

Answers
1 have been paid
2 have ... been
3 felt
4 weren't
5 hasn't been proved
6 have gained
7 have ... been created
8 have got
9 hasn't changed
10 have always been
11 haven't ... done
12 was

Pre-activity (5 minutes)
- Write a controversial statement on the board, e.g. *We have become obsessed with the way we look.* Remind students of the language of opinions, e.g. *I reckon, I'd say, I think so too, I know what you mean, but… etc.*
  Put students into pairs to discuss the statement.
- Have a class feedback session. Establish who agrees with the statement and who disagrees.

Procedure (20 minutes)
- Explain that students are going to complete some statements about different topics to practise different forms of the Present Perfect, and the Past Simple and then have a discussion.
- Give each student a copy of the worksheet. Copy the *TRUE/ MAYBE/NOT TRUE* boxes onto the board. Elicit the missing verb form for number 1 (*have been paid*). Then get a range of students to mark their opinions with a tick in the appropriate box, also adding your own tick.
- Students complete the gapped statements and record their response each time in the same way. Check the answers.
- Put students in pairs or groups of three to compare their responses to the statements. If possible, put students of different nationalities and/or ages together to encourage some lively debate!
- To get students to practise the third person singular, ask them to work with a new partner to talk about their first partner's opinions.

Extension (15 minutes)
- Ask students to choose a statement from p39 that particularly interests them. They prepare a short talk on this topic. Refer them back to SB p107 for language to help them prepare.
- Put students into groups of three or four. Ask them to take turns to give their talks. Encourage questions from the rest of the group.

It's a matter of opinion

1 Footballers _____ (pay) far too much for the last 20 years.

TRUE ☐ MAYBE ☐ NOT TRUE ☐

2 Women _____ always _____ (be) more interested in family life than men.

TRUE ☐ MAYBE ☐ NOT TRUE ☐

3 Life _____ (feel) a lot simpler for my grandparents' generation.

TRUE ☐ MAYBE ☐ NOT TRUE ☐

4 People _____ (not be) interested in celebrity gossip until recently.

TRUE ☐ MAYBE ☐ NOT TRUE ☐

5 Global warming _____ (not / prove) conclusively up to now.

TRUE ☐ MAYBE ☐ NOT TRUE ☐

6 Women _____ (gain) equality with men over the last few years.

TRUE ☐ MAYBE ☐ NOT TRUE ☐

7 The most important inventions in the world _____ all _____ (create) in the USA.

TRUE ☐ MAYBE ☐ NOT TRUE ☐

8 People _____ (get) more and more dependent on technology in recent years.

TRUE ☐ MAYBE ☐ NOT TRUE ☐

9 The structure of the family _____ (not / change) for centuries.

TRUE ☐ MAYBE ☐ NOT TRUE ☐

10 Politicians _____ (always / be) more interested in their own careers than in the people they represent.

TRUE ☐ MAYBE ☐ NOT TRUE ☐

11 Men _____ ever _____ (not / do) their fair share of housework.

TRUE ☐ MAYBE ☐ NOT TRUE ☐

12 The best music and literature in the world _____ (produce) before 1900.

TRUE ☐ MAYBE ☐ NOT TRUE ☐

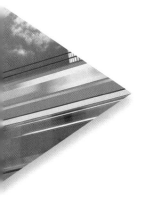

7.2

Loves and hates
LESSON LINK   Unit 7, SB p60

Aim
To talk about how passionate you are about different things

Language
Passions

Skills
Vocabulary, Speaking, and Listening

Materials
One copy of the worksheet per student

Pre-activity (5 minutes)
- Quickly check the language of passions by asking students to think of one thing they love doing, one thing they don't mind doing, and one thing they can't bear doing. Elicit a few answers from different students.

Procedure (15 minutes)
- Explain that students are going talk about their loves and hates.
- Put students into pairs and give each student a worksheet.
- Tell students that at the top of the page are ten expressions for talking about passions and at the bottom of the page are ten topics. Students should take turns to use an expression to talk about one of the topics for 20 seconds e.g.

  I'm not that keen on getting up early on winter mornings because I don't like the dark and it's usually cold as well. I find it much easier in the summer when the mornings are light.

- If students manage to talk on the subject for 20 seconds using an expression from the box, they can tick off that expression on their worksheet. If they can't talk for that long using one of the expressions, they can't tick off a box. The winner is the first person in each pair to tick all the expressions on their worksheet.

Extension (10 minutes)
- Ask students to write down two or three things their partner talked about e.g. *You adore camping because you love the outdoor life.* They read them out to their partner who confirms whether they are accurate or not.

Loves and hates

Use one of the expressions below to talk about the topics 1–10:

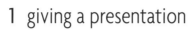

1 giving a presentation

2 getting up early on winter mornings

3 having a lie-in

4 watching a soap opera on TV

5 camping

6 waiting for a bus or train in the rain

7 talking on the phone

8 dressing smartly

9 going to parties

10 spending time with your family/friends

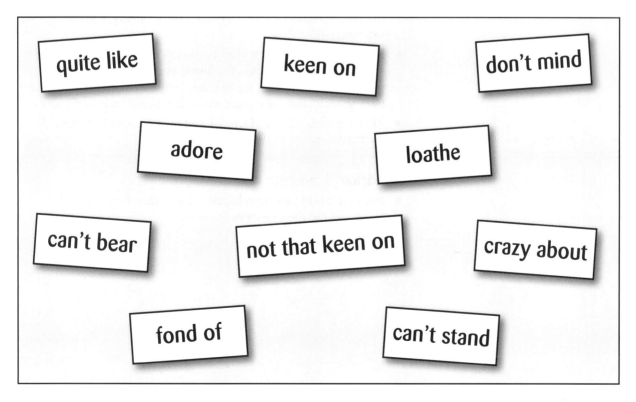

quite like   keen on   don't mind

adore   loathe

can't bear   not that keen on   crazy about

fond of   can't stand

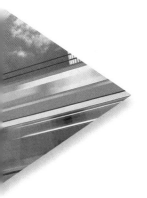

7.3

Reach for the stars
LESSON LINK   Unit 7, SB p61

Aim

To discuss who should be the winner of a reality TV show

Language

Present Perfect and Past Simple

Fluency practice

Skills

Reading, Listening, and Speaking

Materials

One copy of the worksheet on p43 cut up per group of four students

One copy of the worksheets on pp44 and 45 per student

Pre-activity (5 minutes)

- Write the words reality TV shows on the board and the following scale on the board:

  0 ————————————————————— 10
  can't stand   *adore*

  Students come to the board and put a cross on the line that represents their opinion and then explain why.
- Ask students to give brief descriptions of popular reality TV programmes from their own country.

Procedure (30 minutes)

- Explain that students are going to choose the winner of a reality TV programme called *Reach for the stars*. The contestants are four business professionals who are going to take part in a task. The winner will get a highly-paid job in a top firm.
- Put students into groups of four. Give each student a role card and ask them to read it. Point out that the background information is given in note form and that students need to form complete sentences when they describe each character to their classmates.
- Hand out copies of the blank cards on p44. Students take it in turns to describe their character adding as much extra detail as possible, and take notes on the other contestants.
- Hand out a copy of p45 to each student which summarizes the judges' feedback on each contestant. Students read the information.
- Students work in their groups to discuss the feedback and decide who should be the winner. Explain that all the students in each group need to agree on the best candidate. Remind them to think back to each contestant's aim when they assess their performance.
- Elicit students' choice of winner and their reasons in a short feedback session.

Extension (15 minutes)

- Put students in pairs to role play an interview between a TV presenter and the winner of the contest.

B

★ Reach for the stars ★

Contestant Profile

Name: Todd Becker   **Age:** 31   **From:** New York

Background: Worked for top New York marketing agency for five years. Set up own agency three years ago. Now has offices in New York, London, and Shanghai.

Aim: 'I know everything there is to know about marketing. I can sell anything to anyone.'

D

★ Reach for the stars ★

Contestant Profile

Name: Dev Kapoor   **Age:** 30   **From:** Mumbai

Background: Youngest male to get first-class accountancy degree. Became Financial Director of top firm at age of 27. Has run own financial consultancy for two years.

Aim: 'Finance is the most important part of any business. With my knowledge and experience, I can make a huge profit and win the task.'

A

★ Reach for the stars ★

Contestant Profile

Name: Katya Petrov   **Age:** 29   **From:** Moscow

Background: Set up own fashion business at age of 19. Won 'Young Designer of the Year' twice. Has turned three failing businesses into successes.

Aim: 'I'm very creative but I also have a good business head. I'm going to use all my skills to win the task.'

C

★ Reach for the stars ★

Contestant Profile

Name: Abigail Jefferson   **Age:** 28   **From:** London

Background: Youngest female to get first-class MBA. Worked for three of the most successful businesses in the world. Has run own business consultancy for three years.

Aim: 'I'm the best project manager in the business. I'll run any task they give me like clockwork – and I'll win.'

Reach for the stars

Contestant Profile

Name: _____   Age: ____   From: ____

Background:
_____

Aim:
_____

Reach for the stars

Contestant Profile

Name: _____   Age: ____   From: ____

Background:
_____

Aim:
_____

Reach for the stars

Contestant Profile

Name: _____   Age: ____   From: ____

Background:
_____

Aim:
_____

Reach for the stars

Contestant Profile

Name: _____   Age: ____   From: ____

Background:
_____

Aim:
_____

Reach for the stars

Task: To produce, market, and sell an exciting new event planning service

- **Budget:** €1,000
- **Timescale:** 5 days
- **Sales:** Only half the available dates were booked.
- **Profit/Loss:** €150 profit

Team performance

Katya — Creative director

- **Positive:** People loved the cool and exciting ideas for parties, weddings and conferences.
- **Negative:** She didn't pay much attention to deadlines and costs.
- **Comment:** 'Dev is a whizz-kid at finance, but he's just not a team player. In fact, I don't think he likes anybody else in the team.'

Todd — Sales and marketing

- **Positive:** He came up with a clever logo and brand name.
- **Negative:** He took a long time to decide who the target market was.
- **Comments:** 'Abigail was well-organized at the beginning. A bit bossy, maybe. But she did nothing to help on the actual project.'

Abigail — Project manager

- **Positive:** She set up a schedule at the start and gave clear instructions to each team member.
- **Negative:** She failed to check on progress so the team ran out of time.
- **Comments:** 'Todd is extremely creative, but he's so indecisive. He really slowed us down. We didn't have enough time to sell all the sunglasses.'

Dev — Budget control

- **Positive:** He kept a close eye on all aspects of the budget so that they didn't overspend.
- **Negative:** He didn't communicate very well with the rest of the team.
- **Comments:** 'Katya really came up with some brilliant designs. I thought she would be good on the money side, but we only kept to budget because of me.'

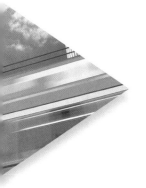

8.1

Aim

To consolidate verb patterns by matching sentence halves in a dominoes game

Language

Verb patterns

Skills

Speaking

Materials

One copy of the worksheet cut up per group of three or four students

Suggested answers

I'll always remember getting my first pay cheque.

I wish I'd managed to pass my driving test last year.

Later this year he's hoping to buy himself a car.

My family is looking forward to having a summer party.

On my way home I always stop to buy my favourite sweets.

When I was a teenager I loved staying out late.

My mum always used to make me finish up all my meals.

My sister is always asking me to lend her money.

At the end of this month I mustn't forget to pay my credit card bill.

I don't think I'll ever finish writing this essay.

For my next holiday I'm thinking of travelling to Hungary.

When I retire I'd love to travel round the world with my wife.

When I fly, I can't help feeling a bit scared.

After this class, I need to get some cash and go shopping.

When I was at school I wasn't much good at drawing and painting.

Before my next test I promise to revise very hard.

In my city it's impossible to park anywhere near the centre.

My brother finds it difficult to talk to strangers.

At the weekend, my mother enjoys spending time with her friends.

I'll always feel sorry for letting my parents down.

Tomorrow you must remember to send your mother a birthday card.

Last class our teacher told us to revise for a test.

People in my city want politicians to lower taxes.

To be greener we need to stop using our cars.

Pre-activity (5 minutes)

- Write the following sentence stems on the board and elicit a range of possible endings:

  I really enjoy (painting).

  I'm thinking of (moving house).

  I forgot (to buy some petrol).

  My doctor advised (me to give up smoking).

  The teacher helped (us understand the question).

  My boss didn't let (the staff leave early).

  I think it's difficult (to work and study at the same time).

Procedure (30 minutes)

- Explain that students are going to play a game to help them remember different verb patterns.

- Put students into groups of three or four and give each group a set of dominoes placed face down on the table.

- Briefly review useful language for playing the game: *Whose turn is it? It's my/your turn. I can't go. I have to miss a turn. Do these cards match? I don't think that's right. Let's check with the teacher. Take another card. I've used all my cards. I'm the winner.*

- Students take five dominoes each and leave the rest in the pile face down.

- The first student puts down a card face up. The second student looks at his/her dominoes and tries to find a card that will match with the verb pattern on one of the sides. If he/she can't go, he/she has to take another card. He/She can put this card down if it matches. Play passes to the next person. The game continues around the group. The first player to get rid of all their dominoes is the winner.

- If a group finishes early, students can ask each other questions using some of the verb patterns on the cards, e.g. *What are you thinking of doing next weekend? Did you forget to do anything important yesterday?*

Extension (10 minutes)

- Students choose and complete five of the sentence stems to make true statements about themselves. Put students in new groups to discuss their ideas.

- Students report back about another member of their group in a short feedback session.

using our cars.	I'll always remember …		to travel round the world with my wife.	When I fly, I can't help …
getting my first pay cheque.	I wish I had managed …		feeling a bit scared.	After this class, I need to …
to pass my driving test last year.	Later this year he's hoping …		get some cash and go shopping.	When I was at school, I wasn't much good …
to buy himself a car.	My family is looking forward …		at drawing and painting.	Before my next test I promise to …
to having a summer party.	On my way home I always stop …		revise very hard.	In my city it's impossible to …
to buy my favourite sweets.	When I was a teenager I loved …		park anywhere in the centre.	My brother finds it difficult to …
staying out late.	My mum used to make me …		talk to strangers.	At weekends my mother enjoys …
finish up all my meals.	My sister is always asking me		spending time with her friends.	I'll always feel sorry for …
to lend her money.	At the end of this month I mustn't forget …		letting my parents down.	Tomorrow you must remember to …
to pay my credit card bill.	I don't think I'll ever finish …		send your mother a birthday card.	Last class our teacher told …
writing this essay.	For my next holiday I'm thinking …		us to revise for a test.	People in my city want politicians …
of travelling round Hungary.	When I retire, I'd love …		to lower taxes.	To be greener we need to stop …

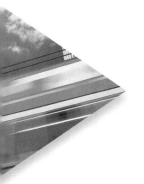

8.2

Aim

To practise a range of numbers by completing a quiz

Language

Numbers, measurements, prices, dates, etc.

Skills

Reading and Speaking

Materials

One copy of the worksheet per students

Answers

1b (auctioned for charity in Qatar in May 2006 for £1.5 million)

2a (a Singapore Airlines flight with the total duration of 18hrs and 35 mins)

3c (estimated number is actually 178)

4b (if you measure through the poles, the circumference is a bit shorter – 40,008 km)

5c (Forbes Traveller gave a ranking of the world's 50 most visited tourist attractions in 2007)

6a (starting price for tickets though Virgin promise to reduce this asap)

7c (Yakutsk is a remote city in Eastern Siberia, population approx 200,000)

8b (BankAmericard, now Visa, also launched a card in the same year)

9a (all airlines differ though flights to the USA often have a higher allowance)

10c (you pay VAT on most goods and services in the UK at the standard rate, 15–17.5%)

Pre-activity (5 minutes)

- Write a large number, a price, a phone number, a distance, and a weight on the board. Ask students to guess what they refer to, e.g. *Is that the population of this city? I think that's your credit card bill for this month, etc.*

Procedure (15 minutes)

- Explain that students are going to complete a quiz to help them remember how to say a range of numbers in English.
- Give students a copy of the worksheet and give them a minute to read through the questions.
- Students decide on the answers to each question in the quiz, working individually.
- Put students in pairs or groups of three to discuss the answers. Explain that they have to agree on their answers to all ten questions.
- Elicit a range of possible answers from the class, asking students to read out the numbers in their answers. Ask students to give reasons for their choices. With competitive groups of students, keep the score to find out which pair/group got the most answers right.
- Ask students which answers they thought were most interesting/ surprising in a brief feedback session.

Extension (15 minutes)

- Students research in pairs and write another number quiz with 4–5 questions. Students then exchange their quizzes with another pair.

It's all about the numbers

Try our quiz and find out of you're number 1 or if you just don't count.

1 What is the world's most expensive mobile phone number?
   a 1234567 **b** 666 6666 **c** 90909090

2 What is the world's longest non-stop scheduled passenger flight?
   a Singapore to New York in 18 hours 35 minutes
   b Buenos Aires to Delhi in 18 hours 40 minutes
   c London to Sydney in 18 hours 45 minutes

3 How many currencies are there across the world?
   a between 50 and 75 **b** between 75 and 100 **c** over 150

4 What is the circumference of the earth around the equator?
   a 400,075.16 km **b** 40,075.16 km **c** 14,075.16 km

5 According to a travel magazine, which is the most visited tourist attraction in the world with over 35 million visitors?
   a the Giza Pyramids, Cairo
   b the Great Wall of China
   c Times Square, New York

6 How much would it cost to book on one of Virgin Galactic's flights into space?
   a $200,000 **b** $20,000 **c** $2,000,000

7 What temperatures would you expect in winter in Yakutsk, the world's coldest city?
   a about minus 24°C **b** about minus 4°C **c** about minus 40°C

8 In which year was the credit card American Express launched?
   a 1928 **b** 1958 **c** 1978

9 What is the average luggage restriction for scheduled flights?
   a 20 kg plus 5g hand luggage
   b 30 kg plus 3g hand luggage
   c 12 kg plus 4g hand luggage

10 If you buy an adult's sweater for £120, how much of the cost is VAT if the rate is 17.5%?
   a £19 **b** £29 **c** £21

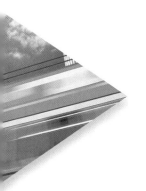

9.1

Talking to my younger self

LESSON LINK   Unit 9, SB p71

Aim

To match sentence halves and then personalize by writing about your own life

Language

Second and third conditionals

might/could/should have

Skills

Reading and Speaking

Materials

One copy of the worksheet per student

Answers

1 f   2 d   3 b   4 e   5 a   6 c

Pre-activity (5 minutes)

- Explain that students are going to practise the third conditional form and then they are going to write their own sentences.
- Give each student the worksheet. Explain that Jenny is looking back on her life and talking about how things could have been different. Ask students to match the two halves of the sentences. Check the answers.

Procedure (20 minutes)

- Tell students an anecdote about a day that started really badly, e.g. *I forgot to set my alarm clock and so I woke up half an hour late. I missed breakfast and ran to the bus stop. I hadn't listened to the news so I didn't know that there was a bus strike. I ended up getting a taxi to work that cost £30 and my boss was angry with me for being late.*
- Write sentence stems on the board and elicit a range of sentences: *If you'd set your alarm clock, (you wouldn't have woken up late). If you'd rung your boss, (he might not have been angry). If you'd cycled to work, (you could have arrived on time).*
- Tell students to look at *My Life* on the worksheet. Explain that students are going to look back on their lives so far and talk about things that could have been different. Ask students to look at the sentence stems. They should write their own examples for the beginning of each sentence next to 1–6.
- Give students time to write their sentences. Put students into pairs and ask them to take it in turns to read out the first part of a sentence and their partner guesses how the sentence is completed e.g.
  A *If I hadn't failed my exams last year, …*
  B *…you wouldn't have had to do them again?*
  A *Yes, that's right.*

Extension (15 minutes)

- Give students the starting point of a story – Henry used to be a millionaire but now he's poor. Ask students to describe how Henry had a lot of money and then lost it. Ask them to write a short letter to the young Henry from the older, wiser, poorer Henry commenting on the episode using the structures from Unit 9.

Jenny's life

1 Jenny is looking back on different aspects of her life. Match the two parts of the sentences to make third conditionals.

1		If I'd gone to a different primary school, ...	**a** I couldn't have bought a flat.
2		If I hadn't rebelled so much at home as a teenager, ...	**b** I might have got a better degree.
3		If I hadn't spent so much time partying at university, ...	**c** I wouldn't have had my lovely son Luc.
4		If I'd worked harder at my languages, ...	**d** I might have had an easier relationship with my parents.
5		If I hadn't saved up all through my twenties, ...	**e** I could have got a job in the diplomatic service.
6		If I hadn't married Tony, ...	**f** I wouldn't have met my two best friends.

Me

2 Use the sentence stems to write sentences about your life.

| 1 If I'd ... | 2 If I'd ... | 3 If I hadn't ... | 4 If I hadn't ... | 5 If I'd ... | 6 If I'd ... |

I would have   I might have

I couldn't have

I wouldn't have   I could have

I would have been able to

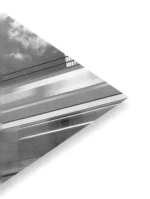

9.2

A question of conscience

LESSON LINK Unit 9, SB p73

Aim

To play a board game to talk about unreal situations in the present and past, and possibility and advice for past situations

Language

Second and third conditionals

might / could / should have

Fluency practice

Skills

Speaking

Materials

One copy of the worksheet per group of three or four students. Each group will need a dice and each student will need a counter

Pre-activity (5 minutes)

- Give an example from your childhood of when you had a guilty conscience and say what you should have done. *I broke my sister's toy but I didn't tell her. I should have been more honest.* Elicit further examples from the class.

Procedure (30 minutes)

- Explain that students are going to play a game to practise sentences with *if* and to comment on questions of conscience.
- Put students into groups of three or four and give each group a copy of the worksheet. Each group will also need a dice and a set of counters.
- Explain how to play the game: students take it in turns to throw the dice and move round the board according to the number they throw. If they land on a square with the beginning of a sentence, they complete the sentence to make it true for themselves, and then continue talking about the topic for 30 seconds. Other students can ask questions or prompt to get more information. If students land on *A question of conscience* square, they read out the situation and then say what the person could/should have done, and what they would have done if they'd been in that situation.
- Students play the game in their groups.
- Elicit any interesting information/opinions that came out of the game in a brief feedback session.

Extension (10 minutes)

- Ask students to work in new groups. Get them to complete some of the sentence stems in writing on strips of paper without writing their name. Students put the strips in a pile, choose one and read it out, and then say who they think wrote it and why.

What would you do?

START ▶

If I needed help with my studies, ...

Things in my country would have been different if ...

What would you do?

A friend found a diamond ring in the street and kept it.

I would have travelled more in my past if ...

If I could invent something new, ...

What would you do?

Your neighbour dented another person's car in your street, but didn't admit it.

If I spoke perfect English, ...

If I hadn't come to class today, ...

What would you do?

Your manager gave promotion to the candidate he/she liked best.

I might move to another country if ...

I think I'd be very happy if ...

What would you do?

A classmate was given a higher exam mark than he/she deserved by mistake.

I wouldn't be surprised if ...

If I hadn't been born in ...,

What would you do?

A friend wasn't truthful on his/her CV, so he/she got an interview.

FINISH

What would you do?

A relative sold a valuable painting that had been in your family for years without asking permission.

I would have enjoyed primary school more if ...

If I'd known when I was younger what I know now, ...

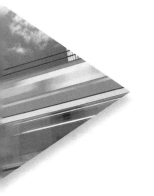

10.1

Hi-tech heroes from history

LESSON LINK   Unit 10, SB p79

Pre-activity (5 minutes)

- Ask students to think of an invention they couldn't live without and one they think is a waste of time/money.
- Elicit a range of examples from the class.

Procedure (30 minutes)

- Explain that students are going to read a short text about an invention/development and then work in groups to present and defend their invention.
- Put students into three groups A, B, and C. Hand out the appropriate text to the students in each group.
- Tell students to read their text and write down key words to help them remember how their item was developed and what its benefits to society in general are. They should not write full sentences.
- Put students in A/B/C groups. Ask students to put their texts away and work from just their notes. Students take it in turns to present their invention and justify why it's the most important, e.g. *The camera is very important to society because it is a way of recording our memories. If it hadn't been invented, people would not have been able to record key events in history.* They should try and get the other two students to accept their opinions.
- Establish which students managed to persuade their classmates to accept their item as the most important.

Extension (15 minutes)

- Students write a set of jumbled instructions for using an everyday invention without naming it. They exchange instructions with a partner and who has to number the instructions and guess what it is.

A Photography

The modern digital photograph is the result of a series of developments rather than a single invention. A French inventor called Joseph Niépce /niːˈjeps/ produced the first photograph around 1824. The problem with his technique was that the image was not permanent and so it soon faded. Another Frenchman, Joseph Daguerre /dæˈɡeə/ later managed to create images that didn't change or fade. The earliest technique that allowed multiple copies of an image was developed by William Fox Talbot, a British inventor. In the late 1800s, the age of photography really took off with the invention of photograph on film.

It's thanks to these early inventors that we can all enjoy photography today. Before photography, the only way to get a picture of yourself was to order a portrait from an artist. Now, almost everyone can record their memories digitally and photos are part of everyday life. Digital cameras have made photographers of us all.

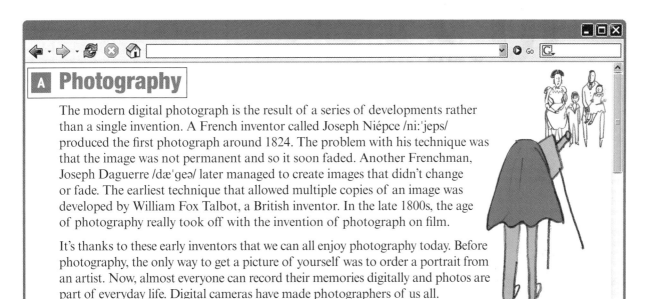

B The printing press

The printing press has had an incredible impact on modern civilization. Some of the earliest examples of printing are from China. The text was carved into wood, stone, or metal, rolled with ink or paint, and then pressed onto parchment or vellum. However, it wasn't until the late 1430s that a German inventor and businessman, Johannes Gutenberg, created a printing press with moveable letters made of wood or metal. Gutenberg's invention meant that text could be printed repeatedly onto paper, and could be changed quickly and easily. In the 1450s, he used his revolutionary system to print a number of bibles in Latin. Although it is not known the exact number of Gutenberg Bibles that were printed, there are still 48 copies in existence today, each one worth millions of pounds.

The invention of the printing press not only made information available to a much bigger section of the population, it also meant that libraries were able to store information at a much lower cost. The printing press started an 'information revolution' in the same way as the Internet today.

C Aspirin

If you get a headache, the easiest thing is to treat yourself with one or two aspirin tablets. Aspirin's key ingredient, an acid that comes from the bark of the willow tree, was first used in ancient Greece in the fourth century B.C. Hippocrates /hɪˈpɒkrətiːz/, who became known as the 'father of medicine', used powder made from the willow bark to treat pain and fever. In the 19th century scientists realized it was the acid in the willow that made the painkiller work but it also gave patients stomach problems. In 1897, Felix Hoffman, a German chemist, improved the remedy while he was trying to find a treatment for his father's arthritis. And so aspirin was developed.

Although everyone knows aspirin as a cure for headaches, it's also used to treat many other serious conditions. Doctors sometimes recommend people at risk of heart attacks to take an aspirin a day, and aspirin is also used to prevent and treat strokes. It's hard to imagine a world where people had to put up with severe pain because painkillers like aspirin were not freely and cheaply available.

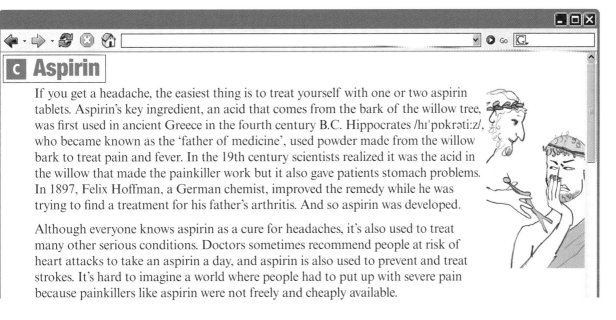

10.2

Aim

To be the first team to match cards and form compound nouns

Language

Compound nouns

Skills

Vocabulary and Speaking

Materials

One copy of the worksheet cut up into cards per group of three or four students

Answers

headache headphones headquarters

sunglasses suncream sunset

credit card birthday card business card

tea bag teacup teatime

briefcase suitcase bookcase

dining room waiting room changing room

hairbrush hairdresser haircut

traffic lights traffic warden traffic jam

antique shop second-hand shop shoe shop

motorway motorbike motor racing

Spider-man postman chairman

wrapping paper toilet paper wallpaper

Pre-activity (5 minutes)

- Write the following words on the board: *brake bag luggage*
  Ask students to supply the headword. Give them a choice of *head hand hair*

Procedure (15 minutes)

- Explain that students are going to play a team game in which they race to match cards and form compound nouns.
- Put students into teams of three or four. Give each team a set of headword cards and ask them to place them face up on the table. Then give the group the other set of cards and ask them to place them face down on the desk. Explain that each card has a word on it that will make a compound with one of the headwords.
- Briefly review useful language for playing the game: *Do these cards match? I don't think that's right. Find another card. Is ... one or two words?*
- Explain that when you shout *Go!* they should turn over the cards and match the compounds correctly as one or two words. Ask each team to choose a student to write their answers. Students should shout *Finished!* as soon as they have matched all the nouns and checked the spelling of their answers.
- Check the answers of the first team to finish. If they are not completely correct, allow the race to continue until one team wins.
- Check the answers with the whole class, including the pronunciation of the compound nouns.

Extension (15 minutes)

- In pairs, students choose five compounds nouns and write a short dialogue using all of them. Alternatively, write sets of nouns for groups of students to work with, e.g.
  – birthday card, wrapping paper, credit card, antique shop, second-hand shop
  – suncream, sunglasses, suitcase, motorway, traffic jam
  Ask students to read out their dialogues to the class.

head	hair	shop	card
sun	traffic	man	case
tea	motor	paper	room

credit	ache	waiting	quarters
brief	glasses	cream	set
dining	shoe	business	second-hand
antique	bag	cup	time
Spider-	suit	book	cut
wrapping	phones	changing	jam
way	brush	dresser	racing
post	lights	warden	bike
wall	toilet	birthday	chair

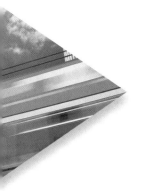

11.1

What on earth is happening?
LESSON LINK   Unit 11, SB p89

Aim
To deduce what is happening in a picture from facial expressions, gestures, and posture

Language
Modal verbs of probability
looks like

Skills
Speaking and Listening

Materials
One copy of each worksheet cut up per pair of students

Pre-activity (10 minutes)

- Demonstrate the activity by holding up your hands in front of you as if you were keying some text on a keyboard. Ask students what they think you are doing, e.g. Y*ou might be using a computer. You could be playing the piano.*

- Briefly review perfect modal forms with *must, might, could* by miming different actions, e.g. *holding your head and grimacing: You must have hurt your head.*

Procedure (25 minutes)

- Explain that students are going to look at two sets of cartoons showing a variety of situations. The first set is called *Now I get it!* because it shows complete scenes and the second set is called *What on earth is happening?* because it shows only the main character in the scene. The background/setting, objects, and other people have been removed. Students are going to look at four *What on earth is happening?* cartoons and use clues to guess what is happening in each picture.

- Divide students into pairs. Give Students A *Now I get it!* cartoons 1–4, *What on earth is happening?* cards 5–8, and *Clue cards* 1–4. Give Students B *Now I get it!* cartoons 5–8, *What on earth is happening?* cards 1–4, and *Clue cards* 5–8. Tell students not to show each other their cards.

- In their pairs, students take it in turns to talk about the cartoons. Student B tells Student A what he/she thinks might be happening/ might have happened in *What on earth is happening?* cartoon 1, e.g. *She might be hiding something from another person. She could have just dialled a number.* Student A reads out the clues on *Clue* card 1 to help Student B make his/her final guess about what is happening, e.g. *She must be entering her PIN into a cash machine.* Student A shows Student B *Now I get it!* card 1 so that he/she can check how close he/she got to the correct answer.

- Students then swap roles and Student A tells Student B what he/she thinks is happening in one of his/her *What on earth is happening?* cards.

- Students continue until all the cards have been used.

Extension (10 minutes)

- In pairs, students create and mime a *What on earth is happening?* scene. The rest of the class guess what they are doing.

Now I get it cards

What on earth is happening cards?

Photocopiable © Oxford University Press

1 Clue card

In this picture, the woman is in the street.

She is trying to get something.

She doesn't want other people to see.

2 Clue card

In this picture, the man is with other people.

They all feel frightened.

What they are looking at isn't real.

3 Clue card

In this picture, the woman isn't enjoying herself.

She shouldn't have gone to where is she.

There's an animal.

4 Clue card

In this picture, the man is working.

He has just dropped something.

Another person is in danger.

5 Clue card

In this picture, the woman is having fun.

She is doing the activity alone.

Some children want to do what she is doing.

6 Clue card

In this picture, the man is outside.

He is trying to do something kind.

Other people want to help.

7 Clue card

In this picture, the woman is in town.

She wants to be first.

There are other people who want what she wants.

8 Clue card

In this picture, the weather is cold.

The man is with a friend.

They are playing.

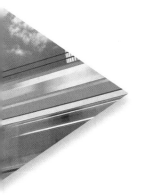

11.2

Aim

To find a path through a maze by choosing the correct pronunciation of forms of *have*

Language

Weak and strong forms: /ə/ /æ/

Skills

Speaking

Materials

One copy of the worksheet per student

Answers

H<u>a</u>ve you ordered yet?

I may h<u>a</u>ve made a mistake

My car h<u>a</u>s been stolen!

You could h<u>a</u>ve let me know earlier.

We must h<u>a</u>ve taken the wrong turning.

How long h<u>a</u>ve you been engaged?

We wouldn't h<u>a</u>ve missed the flight if we'd left on time.

H<u>a</u>ve you been waiting long?

How many books h<u>a</u>s she written?

He shouldn't h<u>a</u>ve lied about his qualifications.

I think you must h<u>a</u>ve made a mistake

H<u>a</u>ve you paid the phone bill yet?

How long h<u>a</u>ve you been looking for a new flat?

He might h<u>a</u>ve gone home already.

I couldn't h<u>a</u>ve done any better.

She might h<u>a</u>ve been delayed in traffic.

What h<u>a</u>ve you been up to recently?

If I'd known about the problem, I would h<u>a</u>ve called you.

What h<u>a</u>ve you done to your hand?

H<u>a</u>s it been raining?

Pre-activity (5 minutes)

- Write the following examples on the board:

  H<u>a</u>ve you h<u>a</u>d a holiday yet this year?

  Yes, we h<u>a</u>ve. We h<u>a</u>d a great time in Italy.

  John h<u>a</u>s left home. He h<u>a</u>sn't lived with his parents for six months.

  Ask *Are the underlined sounds /æ/ or /ə/?* Write the correct symbols above the sounds:

    /ə/   /æ/

  H<u>a</u>ve you h<u>a</u>d a holiday yet this year?

        /æ/   /æ/

  Yes, we h<u>a</u>ve. We h<u>a</u>d a great time in Italy.

   /ə/

  H<u>a</u>s John left home?

        /æ/   /æ/

  Yes, he h<u>a</u>s. He h<u>a</u>sn't lived with his parents for six months.

Procedure (15 minutes)

- Explain that students are going to do a puzzle to practise when *have* is pronounced with a schwa /ə/.

- Give students a copy of the worksheet. Explain that they have to focus on the underlined sound in each example. They have to recognize when *have* is pronounced with /ə/ and find a route from start to finish through the correct squares. They can move horizontally or vertically, but not diagonally.

- Put students into pairs to find the route through the maze. Encourage them to say the sentences aloud and to use pencil for their route in case they make a mistake.

- Check the answers with the class. You may need to drill the pronunciation to help students hear and produce the difference between the weak form /ə/ and the strong form /æ/.

- Ask students if they can see any pattern in the use of the weak form /ə/ and the strong form /æ/. (When *have* is a 'full' verb, e.g. *have a party, have a nice time*, etc., in *have to*, in negative auxiliaries, and in short answers, the pronunciation is usually strong /æ/; as an positive auxiliary verb (*has/have*) and in perfect infinitives, *have* is usually weak /ə/.)

Extension (15 minutes)

- Put students in teams of four to build a dialogue, using as many of the sentences in the maze as possible. The team that uses the most sentences correctly wins and can perform their conversation to the rest of the class.

START

Have you ordered yet?	No, I'm sorry I haven't.	She hasn't been working here for very long.	We had a great time on holiday.	Yes, of course I have.
I may have made a mistake.	My car has been stolen!	You could have let me know earlier.	Have a good weekend!	We're having a test on Friday.
I don't have to work today.	I'll have the prawn risotto, please.	We must have taken the wrong turning.	How long have you been engaged?	Can I have two coffees and a tea, please?
No, he hasn't got here yet.	You have a lot of friends, don't you?	Oh, have you? How interesting!	We wouldn't have missed the flight if we'd left on time.	Have you been waiting long?
Could I have a quick word with you?	No, I haven't. I can't afford them.	What did they have a row about?	I haven't found my keys yet.	How many books has she written?
We haven't got much time before the meeting.	How long have you been looking for a new flat?	Have you paid the phone bill yet?	I think you must have made a mistake.	He shouldn't have lied about his qualifications.
I haven't quite finished it yet.	He might have gone home already.	We have a cancellation this afternoon.	Have here or takeaway?	I have lunch around one o'clock.
Did you have fun at the bowling alley?	I couldn't have done any better.	She might have been delayed In traffic.	Let's have a drink before dinner.	I think I'll have a rest for an hour.
We haven't met his new girlfriend yet.	Yes, we have. It was the best film ever.	What have you been up to recently?	Oh, I have. I went there last year.	Why hasn't the post been delivered yet?
Why do I have to go to bed now?	Jo and Max are having a meeting in the board room.	If I'd known about the problem, I would have called you.	What have you done to your hand?	Has it been raining?

FINISH

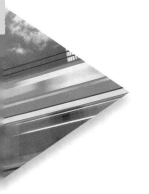

11.3

Aim

To complete a questionnaire about attitudes to life

Language

Phrasal verbs with *out* and *up*

Questions forms

Skills

Reading and Speaking

Materials

One copy of the worksheet per student

Answers

1 working out

2 take up

3 do ... work out

4 ate out

5 have ... fallen out with

6 to make up with

7 breaking up with

8 come up with

9 Do ... eat up

10 do ... save up

11 sort out

12 find out

Pre-activity (10 minutes)

- Review some of the phrasal verbs from Student's Book Unit 11 by dictating sentences and getting students to replace the verb with a phrasal verb with *out* or *up*, e.g.

  <u>Finish</u> your breakfast. (*eat up*)

  You should <u>start doing</u> jogging. (*take up*)

  It's horrible to <u>have an argument</u> with friends. (*fall out*)

  We need to <u>suggest</u> an idea for the party. (*come up with*)

  Let's <u>have dinner in a restaurant</u> tonight. (*eat out*)

  I hope Joe and Ann don't <u>separate</u> forever. (*break up*)

  I need to <u>stop spending</u> to buy a new car. (*save up*)

  I couldn't <u>calculate</u> the answer to the last question. (*work out*)

Procedure (20 minutes)

- Explain that students are going to complete a light-hearted questionnaire about attitudes to life.
- Give each student a copy of the worksheet and ask students to minutes to read through the questions.
- Ask students, in their pairs, to match the illustrations with the topics. Check the answers with the class.
- Students work individually to complete the questions in each section, choosing from the verbs in the box each time and putting them in the correct form. Explain that you will give students time to answer the questions after you have checked the verb forms.
- Students answer the questions, choosing the answers that are closest to their opinion/way of life.
- Students look at the score, work out their total, and read the conclusion.
- Have a brief class feedback session. Ask students if they agree with their conclusion and to say why/why not.

Extension (10 minutes)

- Put students in pairs. Students ask and answer the questions in the questionnaires, this time giving their own answers.
- Have a brief class feedback session. Ask students to report back on anything interesting in their partner's responses.

What's your attitude to life?

Try our fun questionnaire and find out your motto for everyday life …

Free time

> eat out   work out (×2)   take up

1 Do you enjoy _____ the answers to crosswords/ sudoku puzzles?
   a Yes, often.   **b** Not very often.   **c** No, never.

2 Which activity would you like to _____?
   a yoga   **b** skydiving   **c** badminton

3 How often _____ you _____ at the local gym?
   a never   **b** once a week   **c** 3–5 times a week

4 When was the last time you _____ in a restaurant?
   a last month   **b** last week   **c** about 6 months ago

Relationships

> break up with   come up with   make up with   fall out with

5 How often _____ you _____ your parents in your life up to now?
   a Hundreds of times.   **b** Once or twice.   **c** Never.

6 Would you apologize and try _____ a friend after an argument?
   a Yes, always.   **b** No, never.   **c** Sometimes.

7 Would you try to stop your best friend from _____ his/her partner?
   a No.   **b** Of course.   **c** Yes.

8 If you had to organize a school reunion, what plan would you _____?
   a An adventure weekend away.
   b A day trip to the beach.
   c A meal in a local restaurant.

Money

> find out   save up   sort out   eat up

9 _____ you _____ all the food in your fridge before you buy more?
   a No.   **b** Yes.   **c** Usually.

10 How often _____ you _____ for something you want to buy?
   a Never.   **b** Sometimes.   **c** Always.

11 How often do you _____ your clothes, CDs, books etc. to see what you really own?
   a Every six months.
   b About once a year.
   c Never.

12 Do you take time to _____ where the best deals are before you go shopping?
   a No.   **b** Yes.   **c** Sometimes.

Score		
1 a3	b2	c1
2 a3	b1	c2
3 a1	b2	c3
4 a2	b1	c3
5 a1	b2	c3
6 a3	b1	c2
7 a1	b3	c2
8 a1	b2	c3
9 a1	b3	c2
10 a1	b2	c3
11 a3	b2	c1
12 a1	b3	c2

What it means

1–12   Your motto is 'Live for today.'
You are a very spontaneous person and you live life to the full. But you sometimes forget about others and you are not very good at managing money. Try to think about your future a bit more, especially with relationships and planning your finances.

13–24   Your motto is 'Moderation in all things.'
You take a balanced view of life. You know how to have fun, but you also think of others. You think about your future and you look after your finances. You could be a bit more spontaneous sometimes and just follow your heart.

25–36   Your motto is 'Plan for tomorrow.'
You are quite a cautious person who thinks a lot about the future. You dislike problems with relationships. Try not to plan everything in life and just go with the flow sometimes. Remember that today is as important as tomorrow.

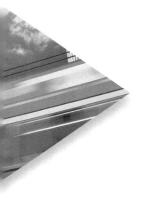

12.1

Aim

To role-play presenters/correspondents on the news programme of a new TV channel

Language

Reporting

Fluency

Skills

Writing and Speaking

Materials

One copy of the worksheet cut up per group of six students

Filming idea

If you have access to a video camera, you might want to film the news programmes and show them to the class in the next lesson. You could then stop the film, as appropriate, to do some error correction.

Pre-activity (5 minutes)

- Write an example of a TV news headlines on the board e.g.
  The Russians break the latest space record.
  Ask students: *What tense is used?* (Present Simple). *Why are the headlines short?* (to attract the listeners' attention and make them want to find out more in the main news story)

Procedure (30 minutes)

- Explain that students are going to role play members of a news team on a new channel called *Headway TV* which is trying to get good viewer ratings.
- Put students into groups of 4 and give each one a role card.
- Give students time to read through their role. Deal with any vocabulary queries they may.
- The correspondents describe their breaking news to the main presenter. He/She notes the stories down and then selects three or four of the most important. He/She then writes short headlines, decides on which order to read them in, and also thinks of possible questions to ask when he/she interviews each correspondent.
- Meanwhile students B–D should think of details they can add to their news stories, e.g. names of people and places, numbers and figures, other quotations from people involved, etc.
- Each group must then decide on the order the stories will appear in the news programme. Tell students that they should not refer to their notes all the time.
- If possible, rearrange the classroom to make the news programme appear more realistic, e.g. a presenter's desk, an area for the correspondents to stand and present their stories.
- Students role-play their news programmes to the class. Monitor and note any errors to be dealt with in a later lesson. If appropriate, allow students to vote for the best news team.

Extension (15 minutes)

- Ask students to write a newspaper article about their area of news. Students who played the presenter can write about a current news story they have seen on TV or read about.

Rolecard A

You are the main presenter.

It's your job to find out the breaking news stories from the rest of the team, select the most important stories, and write the headlines for the start of the news bulletin.

You also have to interview each of the correspondents during their update to find out information that the public would like to know.

Don't forget to:

- greet the viewers.
- introduce each correspondent clearly.
- provide the links between each section.
- give a summary of the main stories at the end.

Rolecard B

You are the domestic news correspondent.

Tell the news presenter your breaking news so he/she can select and write the headlines.

- Breaking news: transport grinds to halt in winter freeze; should transport minister quit?

Then prepare notes for your domestic news update. Use the information below and add ideas of your own. Report the quotations in a suitable way.

- Update: chaos on roads; weather has affected daily commute to work/school; hundreds of schools closed
- Head Teacher: 'The Transport Minister just hasn't dealt with the problem. I feel he should resign.'
- Member of public: 'Why weren't the roads prepared before the bad weather?'

Rolecard C

You are the international news correspondent.

Tell the news presenter your breaking news so he/she can select and write the headlines.

- Breaking news: forest fires hit Australia; international drug traffickers arrested

Then prepare notes for your international news update. Use the information below and add ideas of your own. Report the quotations in a suitable way.

- Update: huge area of southern Australia affected by forest fires – hundreds of people forced to leave homes; 40 people arrested in one of biggest drug rings; climate change talks continue in Geneva
- Member of public: 'Something must be done about people who start fires deliberately!'
- Police Officer: 'This will mean far fewer drugs out on the streets'

Rolecard D

You are the sports correspondent.

Tell the news presenter your breaking news so he/she can select and write the headlines.

- Breaking news: world's first £50-million footballer; young athlete sets track record

Then prepare notes for your sports news update. Use the information below and add ideas of your own. Report the quotations in a suitable way.

- Update: young African player been signed to top London club for £50m – fans angry at ticket price rise; 14-year-old sets new record in 5,000m
- Fan: 'It's not fair. I'm going to have to give up my season ticket!'
- Athlete: 'I'm surprised I won, but it's a great feeling.'

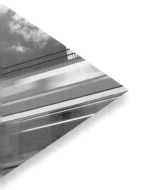

12.2

Aim

To play a board game to review the language of the course

Language

Target structures and vocabulary from the course

Fluency practice

Skills

Speaking and Listening

Materials

One copy of the board game and the cards cut up per group of three or four students. Each group will need a dice and each student will need a counter

Hurdles

A How long have you been studying here? **B** Since June

They asked me where I worked.

My boss told me to finish the report.

I'd have come to the party if you'd told me about it.

Is taking photos allowed in the museum?

They've had a row and have stopped speaking to each other.

A How's school? **B** Fine. I'm really enjoying this term.

I'm not free tomorrow. I'm revising.

I'll always remember passing my driving test.

I might have left my wallet at home.

A What's your new teacher like?

B Very nice and friendly.

It was raining when I walked home.

A Can I help you? **B** I'm being served, thank you.

She was brought up by her dad.

I don't think people will live in space.

The interview was quite informal.

The class worked really hard.

I'm not very keen on sports.

You shouldn't have let the dog out.

Please slow down. You could have killed us back there.

The car has a big scratch on its bonnet.

Everything was covered in dust after the storm.

She can't be English. She had an American accent.

Don't accuse me of stealing.

Pre-activity (5 minutes)

- Ask students to think about the progress they have made since the start of the course. Elicit examples of things students think they have done well and things they think they need to work on further. Establish students' priorities for their next course.

Procedure (30 minutes)

- Explain that students are going to play a board game to review some of the language they have covered in the course.

- Put students into groups of three or four. Give each group a copy of the board game, a set of hurdle cards placed faced down, and a set of *Challenge* cards placed face down in three piles: bronze, silver, and gold. Each group with also need a dice and a set of counters.

- Students take it in turns to throw the dice and move round the board. They will land on one of three types of square:

  Hurdle – the player picks up a hurdle card and if he/she can correct the error in the sentence, he/she stays on that square; if not, he/she goes back a square.

  Challenge – the player chooses the level of challenge he/she wants. If he/she does the challenge successfully, he/she goes forward one square for bronze, two for silver, and three for gold. If the player fails to do the challenge, he/she stays on that square.

  Bonus/penalty squares – the player moves back/forward according to the instructions

  The player to reach FINISH first is the winner.

Extension (10 minutes)

- Ask students to brainstorm a list of ways of keeping their English going until they start their next course. Elicit examples and get students to agree on eight techniques/strategies for keeping up their English. Get students to produce an agreed checklist of techniques along with a timetable to say when/how often they should be done.

MEDAL CARDS

Bronze
Find the words that don't rhyme.
street meat great beat
goes nose lows does
phone son won done

Silver
Can you remember the following?
• Two objects you use in DIY
• Two objects you use when camping
• Three ways of cooking food

Gold
Talk for sixty seconds about your extended family.

Bronze
Say four things about your childhood with these verbs:
(not) have to
(not) be allowed to

Silver
How do you spell these words?
/ˈfɑːrɪn/   /ˈɑnɪst/
/klaɪm/   /ˈneɪbə/

Gold
Talk for sixty seconds about jobs and work in your town.

Bronze
Complete the ways of making suggestions to meet.
I … wondering if we … meet?
What … on Sunday morning?
Why … meet in the main square?

Silver
Make two sentences that show different meanings of each of these phrasal verbs.
take off
pick up
get through

Gold
Talk for sixty seconds about a time when you made an embarrassing mistake or had a clumsy accident.

Bronze
What can you buy in these departments of a store?
Give one example for each department.
• stationery   • kitchenware
• toiletries   • leather goods

Silver
Describe your best friend (looks and personality).

Gold
Talk for sixty seconds about the rules your school has/had.

Bronze
Complete the sentences about your work/studies to make them true for you.
I … never …, I … already …,
I … just …, I … last year.

Silver
Complete the sentences to make them true for you.
I'm looking forward to …
I find it difficult …
I mustn't forget …
I'm quite good at …

Gold
Talk for sixty seconds about what your city will be like in 50 years' time.

Bronze
Mime these actions:
climb a ladder
hit a nail with a hammer
blow up a balloon
lick an ice-cream
kick a football

Silver
Make pairs of sentences with each set of verbs.
win / beat
rob / steal
borrow / lend
buy / pay

Gold
Talk for sixty seconds about something you feel passionate about.

Bronze
Complete the sentences with a suitable modal verb.
They're speaking Portuguese. They … be from Portugal or Brazil.
She … be at home. She's on holiday in Rome.

Silver
Report a short conversation that you had yesterday.

Gold
Talk for sixty seconds about the pros and cons of technology.

HURDLE CARDS

A How long are you studying here? **B** Since June.	I'll always remember to pass my driving test.	The class worked really hardly.
They asked where did I work.	I might of left my wallet at home.	I'm not very keen of sports.
My boss told me that I finish the report.	**A** How is your new teacher? **B** Very nice and friendly.	You shouldn't have leave the dog out.
I'd come to the party if you'd told me about it.	It rained when I walked home.	Please slow down. You would have killed us back there.
Do you allowed to take photos in the museum?	**A** Can I help you? **B** I'm served, thank you.	The car had a big scratch on it's bonnet.
They've had a row and have stopped speaking to themselves.	She was brought after by her dad.	All was covered in dust after the storm.
A How's school? **B** Fine. I really enjoy this term.	I think people won't live in space.	She mustn't be English. She had an American accent.
I'm not free tomorrow. I will revise.	The interview was quite unformal.	Don't accuse me for stealing.

Challenge Bronze, Silver, or Gold?

Hurdle

Challenge Bronze, Silver, or Gold?

Hurdle

You've forgotten a lot of vocabulary. Go back one square.

Challenge Bronze, Silver, or Gold?

Hurdle

Hurdle

Hurdle

Challenge Bronze, Silver, or Gold?

Challenge Bronze, Silver, or Gold?

You've made a lot of progress this term. Move forward two squares.

Hurdle

START

FINISH

Hurdle

Hurdle

Hurdle

Hurdle

You've been revising hard. Move forward two squares.

Challenge Bronze, Silver, or Gold?

Hurdle

Hurdle

Challenge Bronze, Silver, or Gold?

Hurdle

Challenge Bronze, Silver, or Gold?